THE AMERICAN PEOPLE

The American People In Colonial New England

Edited by
JAMES AXTELL

Pendulum Press, Inc.

West Haven, Connecticut

Clothbound Edition ISBN 0-88301-082-8 Complete Set
0-88301-085-2 This Volume

Paperback Edition ISBN 0-88301-066-6 Complete Set
0-88301-069-0 This Volume

Library of Congress Catalog Card Number 72-95867

Published by
Pendulum Press, Inc.
The Academic Building
Saw Mill Road
West Haven, Connecticut 06516

Printed in the United States of America

Cover Design by Dick Brassil, Silverman Design Group

CONTENTS

ABOUT THE EDITOR

James Axtell, the recipient of a B.A. degree from Yale University and a Ph.D. from Cambridge University, has also studied at Oxford University and was a postdoctoral fellow at Harvard University. Mr. Axtell has taught history at Yale and is currently Associate Professor of Anglo-American History at Sarah Lawrence College. He is on the editorial board of *History of Education Quarterly* and has been a consultant to the American Council of Learned Societies. He has published several articles and reviews and is the author of a forthcoming book, *The School upon a Hill: Education and Society in Colonial New England.*

ACKNOWLEDGMENTS

Grateful acknowledgment is made to the authors and publishers who granted permission to reprint the following selections:

Diary of Ebenezer Parkman, from *Proceedings* of the American Antiquarian Society, vols. 29, 71-73. Reprinted by permission.

Diary of Samuel Sewell, from *Collections* of the Massachusetts Historical Society, fifth series, vols. 6-7. Reprinted by permission.

"Families in Colonial Bristol, Rhode Island," vol. 25, pp. 40-57. Copyright 1968. Reprinted by permission of John Demos and the *William and Mary Quarterly*.

Four Generations: Population, Land, and Family in Colonial Andover, Massachusetts, by Philip Greven. Copyright© by Cornell University Press. Reprinted by permission.

Journal-letters of Esther Burr. Courtesy The Bienecke Rare Book and Manuscript Library, Yale University.

A Little Commonwealth, by John Demos. Copyright ©1970 by Oxford University Press, Inc. Reprinted by permission.

Of Plymouth Plantation, by William Bradford; edited by Samuel Eliot Morison. Copyright© Alfred A. Knopf, Inc. Reprinted by permission of the publisher.

Publications of the Colonial Society of Massachusetts, vol. 15, from the records of Harvard College. Reprinted by permission of the Colonial Society of Boston.

Travels Through the Middle Settlements, by Rev. Andrew Burnaby. Published by Cornell University Press. Reprinted by permission.

Winthrop Papers, Massachusetts Historical Society. Reprinted by permission.

FOREWORD

The American People is founded on the belief that the study of history in the schools and junior levels of college generally begins at the wrong end. It usually begins with abstract and pre-digested *conclusions*—the conclusions of other historians as filtered through the pen of a textbook writer—and not with the primary sources of the past and unanswered *questions*—the starting place of the historian himself.

Since we all need, use, and think about the past in our daily lives, we are all historians. The question is whether we can be skillful, accurate, and useful historians. The only way to become such is to exercise our historical skills and interests until we gain competence. But we have to exercise them in the same ways the best historians do or we will be kidding ourselves that we are *doing* history when in fact we are only absorbing sponge-like the results of someone else's historical competence.

Historical competence must begin with one crucial skill—the ability to distinguish between past and present. Without a sharp sense of the past as a different time from our own, we will be unable to accord the people of the past the respect that we would like to receive from the people of the future. And without according them that respect, we will be unable to recognize their integrity as individuals or to understand them as human beings.

A good sense of the past depends primarily on a good sense of the present, on experience, and on the imaginative empathy to relate ourselves to human situations not our own. Although most students have had a relatively brief experience of life and have not yet given full expression to their imaginative sympathies, they do possess the one essential prerequisite for the study of history—the lives they have lived from birth to young adulthood. This should be the initial focus of their study of the past, not remotely adult experiences to which they cannot yet relate, such as politics, diplomacy, and war.

Thus the organizing perspective of this series is the universal life experiences that all people have: being born, growing up, loving and marrying, working and playing, behaving and misbehaving, worshipping, and dying. As only he could, Shakespeare portrayed these cycles in *As You Like It* (Act II, scene vii):

> All the world's a stage,
> And all the men and women merely players.
> They have their exits and their entrances;
> And one man in his time plays many parts,
> His acts being seven ages. At first the infant,
> Mewling and puking in the nurse's arms.
> And then the whining school-boy, with his satchel
> And shining morning face, creeping like snail
> Unwillingly to school. And then the lover,
> Sighing like furnace, with a woeful ballad
> Made to his mistress' eyebrow. Then a soldier,
> Full of strange oaths, and bearded like a pard;
> Jealous in honour, sudden and quick in quarrel,
> Seeking the bubble reputation
> Even in the cannon's mouth. And then the justice,
> In fair round belly with good capon lined,
> With eyes severe and beard of formal cut,
> Full of wise saws and modern instances;
> And so he plays his part. The sixth age shifts
> Into the lean and slipper'd pantaloon,
> With spectacles on nose and pouch on side;
> His youthful hose, well saved, a world too wide
> For his shrunk shank; and his big manly voice,
> Turning again toward childish treble, pipes
> And whistles in his sound. Last scene of all,
> That ends this strange eventful history,
> Is second childishness, and mere oblivion,
> Sans teeth, sans eyes, sans taste, sans everything.

These are experiences to which any student can relate and from which he can learn, simply because they surround him daily in his home, community, and not least, school.

There is an additional reason for focussing on the universal life cycle. If history is everything that happened in the past, obviously some things were and are more important than others. Until fairly recently the things historians have found important have been the turning points or *changes* in history—"great" men and "great" events. But recently, with the help of anthropologists, historians have come to a greater awareness of the importance of stability and inertia, of *non*-change in society. For every society—and therefore its history—is a mixture of change and stability, of generally long periods of fixity punctuated now and then by moments of modification and change.

The major reason for the stability of society is the conservative bent of human behavior and ideals, the desire to preserve, hold, fix, and keep stable. People acquire habits and habits impede change. The habits people acquire are the common ways the members of a society react to the world—how they behave and feel and think in common—which distinguish them from other societies and cultures. So at bottom history is about ordinary people, how they did things alike and together that gave continuity and durability to their society so that it could change to meet new circumstances without completely losing its former identity and character.

America is such a society and *The American People* is an attempt to provide representative selections from primary sources about the lives and habits of ordinary people in periods of history that are usually known in textbooks for their great changes.

Since the experience of each student is the only prerequisite for the study of primary sources at the first level, annotations and introductory material have been reduced to a minimum, simply enough to identify the sources, their authors, and the circumstances in which they were written.

But the remains of the past are mute by themselves. Many sources have survived that can tell us what happened in the past and why, but they have to be questioned properly to reveal their secrets. So by way of illustration, a number of questions have been asked in each chapter, but these should be supplemented by the students whose experiences and knowledge and interests are, after all, the flywheel of the educational process. Although the questions and sources are divided into chapters, they should be used freely in the other chapters; the collection should be treated as a whole. And although most of the illustrative questions are confined to the sources at hand, questions that extend to the present should be asked to anchor the acquired knowledge of the past in the immediate experience of the present. Only then will learning be real and lasting and history brought to life.

INTRODUCTION

It is one of the sustaining ironies of our history that the first Americans were Indians and Englishmen. In the close familiarity of the present, we are apt to forget that the first white settlers of colonial America were the cultural heirs of Elizabethan and Stuart England, not the red-blooded American Revolutionaries of fame and fable.

The people who settled New England were religious Puritans predominately from the cloth-weaving eastern counties of England known as East Anglia. Beginning in 1620 and rising to a crescendo in the Great Exodus of the 1630s, they came to the New World seeking freedom to worship God in their own way, free from what they considered the unscriptural restrictions of the Church of England under its stern patriarch, Archbishop William Laud. They had few differences with the doctrines of the mother Church, which they continued to regard with filial devotion, but they did object to certain of its ceremonies and its administration of discipline. The English Church, they felt, had not been sufficiently "purified" of its Catholic excesses when it was finally converted to Calvinistic Protestantism under Queen Elizabeth. Their criticism—often strident and full of righteous zeal—earned for them the enmity of the episcopal hierarchy, and many Puritan ministers, followed by whole parishes of the faithful, were "hounded out of the land."

After an initial flirtation with Holland, the Puritans selected New England for the site of their "City upon a Hill", a community of godliness that would serve as a beacon of hope to a Europe festering with war, famine, pestilence, and imminent destruction. Believing themselves to be in a special relationship with God, they attempted to fashion a society based on order and harmony so as to avoid the

13

civil and religious strife that had wracked the mother country. The grandeur of their vision and the measure of their success are as important to the history of the American people as their human failings. It is to both these facets of their ''errand into the wilderness'' that this book is devoted.

I. BIRTH

Birth in any culture is a time of hope as well as danger, and colonial New England was no exception. Did New English parents hope for a boy or a girl? Why? Is there any evidence that one was regarded as inferior to the other, even before birth? (See chapter 7, p. 5) Did parents have any choice in the matter of sex? Were boy and girl babies treated any differently at birth? Was this treatment medically necessary or only culturally desirable? How dangerous was childbirth for the babies? Was the primitive wilderness of New England more or less healthy than the civilized towns of the 18th century? Why? Was childbirth dangerous to mothers? Who delivered babies? Were they competent and qualified? How do you know? Were they always necessary? Was the process of having a baby much different than it is today? What are some of the differences? How can you find out?

When the Puritans came to New England, they brought with them a knowledge of childbirth gained from years of folk practice and occasional medical advice. The most popular book on the delivery and care of children in 17th-century England was Child-Birth; or, The Happy Deliverie of Women *by Jacques Guillemeau (1550-1613), chirurgeon to the French king. Translated from the French original several times, the book was at once a summary of the accepted practices of the day and the most advanced obstetrical advice to be had in contemporary Europe. The following passages occur on pp. 8-12 and 86-100 of the London edition of 1612.*

THE SIGNES WHEREBY TO KNOW WHETHER A WOMAN
BE WITH CHILD OF A BOY OR A WENCH.

Having shewne the meanes to know whether a woman be truely
conceived, it will not be from the purpose to handle this question for
the satisfaction of some curious minds, who as soone as the
Chirurgion hath given his censure that a woman is with child, de-
maunds presently of him whether it will be a boy, or a wench? But as
it is very hard to know at the first whether the woman be with child
or no, so by great reason must it needs be farre more difficult to
discerne, and distinguish the difference of the sexe, and to determine
whether it will be a boy or a wench.

I know there are some that boast they can certainely do it, but for
the most part it hapneth rather by chance, then through either arte or
skill. And for proofe thereof, I have shewed them a child newly come
from the mothers wombe, onely laying my hand upon the privie
parts, yet durst they not be so bold as give their opinion thereof, saying, that it were more easie to judge of it when it was in the wombe,
seeing that from thence might be gathered many evident signes: but
wee must account the greatest part of them to be uncertaine, as we
have formerly said. Neverthelesse, to distinguish the Male from the
Female we will presently shew all the marks which we ever knew, or
could observe, either out of the ancient, or moderne writers.

And first of all, yong women commonly are with child rather of a
boy then of a wench, because they be hoter then the elder women,
which was observed by *Aristotle*, who saith farther, that if an aged
woman which never had children before, chance to conceive, one
may be sure it will be a wench. The like hapneth (as some write) to
women, which conceive when the winde is in the South, who for the
most part bring forth daughters, and when the Northwind bloweth,
sonnes.

Hippocrates saith, that a woman which goeth with a boy hath a
good colour, for a woman in her case, but if it be of a wench, she will
have a worse complexion. Likewise if the right breast be harder and
firmer, the nipple hard, red, and more eminent, the milke white and
thicke, which being milked or spirtled against a sleek-stone, or some
such smooth thing, continues in a round forme like a pearle, and
being cast even into water it dissolveth not, but sinks directly to the
bottome: and if you make a cake with the said milke and flower, and
in the baking it continues firme, and close, it is a signe the woman is

with child of a boy. Againe, she that goeth with a boy, hath the right side of her belly bigger, and more copped, and there the child stirreth oftenest. This motion commonly at sixe weeks is scarse sensible, but at two months and a halfe more manifest. The Male child lyeth high above the Navell by reason of his heate, and the Female at the bottome of the belly, because of her coldnes and weight. They which be with child of a boy are more quicke and nimble in all their actions, and be in better health of body, without being subject to many infirmities, which commonly happen to women with child of a wench.

Avicen observeth these signs, that a woman with child of a boy hath the pulse of her right side stronger, higher, and thicker, then that of the left: she will reach out her right hand rather then her left, and in going she wil alwayes set forth the right foote formost: her right brest is bigger then the left, and the right eye greater, brighter, and more sparkling: and if a woman about her last months have any great sicknesse, or any throwes, without being deliverd, it is some likelyhod that she is with child of a boy, since the male child is faster tied and bound then the female, because the ligaments which hold and fasten him are stronger and dryer then they that bind and support a wench.

A woman which is with child of a daughter hath a pale, heavy, and swarth countenance, a melancolique eye: she is wayward, fretfull, and sad: she beares in her face as *Hippocrates* saith, *Maculam solarem*, that is to say, her face is spotted with red, like those who have been much in the sunne: her left brest is bigger then the right; and the top of the nipple blacke. The milke which comes forth of her brests is blewish, thin, and watrish: her belly is flat; and she feeles her burthen move on the left side, and that, not before the fourth moneth: the veines of her thighes, and groine, are bigger, and more knottie on the left side then on the right. An honest Gentlewoman assured me that she had made triall of this receipt, which is, to take an equall quantitie of Claret wine, and of urine made in the morning, put them together into a glasse, and let them stand a whole day, if there appeare in the bottome a grosse cloud, thicke like to Beanebroth, it is a signe the woman is with child of a boy, if it appeare in the middest, it is signe of a wench, if there be nothing found in the bottome but the ordinary residence of urine, it shewes she is not with child at all.

Heere will it not be beside our purpose to set downe what *Hippocrates* writes in his booke *de superfatatione*, of the meanes how to get a man or woman-child. He that wil (saith he) beget a sonne, must know his wife as soone as her courses are stayed, and then try the utmost of his strength; but if he desire to get a daughter, then must he companie with his wife a good while after her courses, or at that time when she hath them: and beside, he must tye his right stone as hard as he can endure it; and when he would have a sonne, he must tye the left. But *Aristotle* seemes wrongfully to blame this worthie man, when he sayth, that the generation of Males or Females depends of the strength of the feed, and not of the stones, the use whereof he saith, is not for generation. But experience teacheth us the contrary, for the countreymen when they would have a Bull beget a Cow-Calfe, or a Bull-Calfe, they tye the right stone for the one, and the left for the other.

WHAT MUST BEE OBSERVED, WHEN THE WOMAN
FEELES HER SELFE, NEARE HER TIME.

The time of delivery being at hand, the woman is to prepare her selfe in this manner. She must presently send for the Midwife, and her keeper, it being better to have them about her too soon, then too late; for there be some women that are delivered sodainely without the helpe of any one, although they have beene long in their first labour.

In the meane time, she must have a little bedde provided her, like a pallet, which must bee of a reasonable bignes, strong and firme, and also of an indifferent height (as well for her owne commodity, as the Midwives, and others that shal be present about her, to helpe her, in her labour) and it must be so set & placed, that they may conveniently come and go round about her, it must be placed far from any doore, and somwhat neere the fire. Let it also be conveniently furnished with beds & good store of linnen that they may be often changed, as neede shall require. And likewise there must bee laid crosse the beds feete, a peece of wood, for the woman to rest her feet upon, that so she may have the more strength when she bendeth her legs, as we will shew heereafter.

As soone as she feeles herselfe stirred and provoked with throwes and paines, which are usuall in this case, it were good for her to walke up and down the chamber, and then lay her selfe down warm in her bed: and then againe afterwards to rise up and walke, expecting till the water bee gathered, and the Matrice be opened: for to keep her selfe so long in her bed, would bee very tedious and painfull. Yet it may chance, that being in bed shee may take some rest and have a little slumber, and so by this meanes the mother may gather more strength, & the child be the better inabled to come at the time, which God hath appointed it, and also the waters will be the better prepared & gathered.

They may give her, if the labour be long, a little broth, or the yelke of an egge with some butter, and bread, and also a little wine and water.

It is very certaine, that all women are not delivered after one fashion: for some are delivered in their bed; others sitting in a chaire, some standing being supported and held up by the standers by: or else leaning upon the side of a bed, table or chaire; others kneeling being held up by the armes. But the best and safest way, is; to be delivered in their bed, (the which I advise them to) the midwife, and assistants, as her kinfolkes, friends, and keepers, observing this that followes.

First the woman must be laid flat upon her back, having her head raised somwhat high, with a pillow under her backe that it bow 'not: and under her buttocks and *os sacrum*, let her have another pretty big pillow, that thereby those parts may bee somewhat lifted up: for a woman that sinketh down into the bed can never be well delivered; and therefore the well placing of them is of great consequence. Let her thighs and knees be stretcht forth and laide abroad one from another: and her legs bowed and drawn upward, having her heels & the soles of her feet, leaning hard against the peece of wood, which is laid crosse the bedde for this purpose.

About some they put a swath foure times doubled under their backe, and hinder parts, which comes round about them: this swath must be a foot broad, & better, and so long, that it may be held by two women, standing on each side of the bed, there with to lift up the woman in travaile a litle, pulling it gently towards them, & chiefly when her throws come upon her. For this raising or lifting up doth much refresh her, and makes her endure her throws with more ease.

Beside the two women that hold the swath, there must be two more of her friends or kinsfolks, to take her by the hands, thereby to clinsh or crush them when her throws come, and the other hand they must hold on the top of her shoulders, that she rise not upward too much, and that she may the better straine her selfe, for oftentimes as shee thrusts her feete hard against the peece of wood, which is put crosse the bed, she raiseth her self upward. Sometime I have bid one of the women that stand by to presse gently with the palme of her hand the upper parts of the belly, stroking the child downward by little and little, the which pressing did hasten the delivery, and made them endure the throws better, and with more ease.

The woman in travaile being thus placed, must take a good heart, and straine her selfe as much as she can, when her throws come upon her, making them double and increase, by holding in her breath and stopping her mouth, and forming her selfe, as though she would go to the stoole, which is much fitter for her to doe then to lye crying and lamenting.

Aristotle hath well observed, that those women, which draw their breath upward, are delivered with much paine, because they make the Midrife rise up, which in this businesse, should rather be depressed, and kept downe. It is very fit indeede, that she take some ease and respite, not forcing her selfe much for every little pang that happens, which she may gather all into one, thereby to make them availeable; when time shall serve.

If she weare about her necke an Eagles stone, loadstone, the skinne of an Urus or wild Oxe or the like, which might keepe backe the child, let them be taken away, and tied to her thighs.

But above all things she must be obedient to all that is commanded her, either by her kinsfolks, and friends, or by the Midwife. Likewise she must be patient in her sicknesse, calling uppon God for helpe, since it concernes both her own life, and the childs, and shee must call to mind, that hee hath said with his owne mouth, *That the woman should bring forth with labour and paine*. For it would bee a rare thing to see a woman delivered without any paine. *Medeain Euripides* saith, *That shee had rather dye twice in the warres, then to be once delivered of a child*.

THE OFFICE AND DUTY OF A MIDWIFE, FOR THE FIRST TIME, SHE MUST OBSERVE IN THE TRAVAILE.

The Woman that is ready to be delivered being thus placed and laid in her bedde, must have the Midwive neere unto her: who ought first to aske of her woman, whether shee hath gone her full time, and bee ready to bee delivered; and at what time shee conceived; then must shee handle her belly, and marking it well, consider diligently whether the upper parts seeme as if they were empty, and fallen, and the nether parts very bigge and full: which sheweth that the child is sunke downe. Beside, she must aske her, whether shee have any paines, and in what manner they bee, where they begin, and where they end: and whether they bee little or great, and frequent: whether they begin at the backe, running downe all along the belly, without staying at the Navell: and chiefly if they run along the groine, and end in the bottom of the belly inwardly (that is in the inner necke of the womb) then it is a signe that she begins to fall in travaile. And for the more assurance, let the Midwife thrust up her hand, being first annointed, either with fresh butter, hogs grease, or some other ointment, which heereafter shall be set downe. And if she perceive that both the inner, and outward orifice of the wombe, be dilated and opened, it is a signe she begins to be in travail, especially if there flow or come forth by the said passage, any slime, or water: the which doe foreshew, that the birth is at hand, as *Hippocrat*. saith, which if they be pale, it signifies for the most part, it will be a wench: and if it be reddish that it is a sonne. Now this slime commeth by the dilatation of the inner orifice, and from the membrane, that doth wrap and infold the child, which begins to breake. And also by reason of the vessels, and tyes which are loosened from the sides of the wombe the which may be perceived by the waters which will swell, shewing like a bubble, or rather like a bladderfull of water. And when the water begins to be thus gathered, there is no doubt to be made, but that the woman is in travail: *Hippocrates* doth observe three sorts of humors, that flow in the time of their travaile: the first, is slimy: the second reddish: the third is the water wherein the child swimmeth, and heere endeth the first time, which the midwife must observe.

OF THE SECOND TIME THAT THE MIDWIFE MUST OBSERVE.

When the waters are in this sort gathered together, by meanes of the throwes, which come by little and little: then the Midwife must place her selfe conveniently neere unto the woman, sitting in a chaire somewhat lower then the bed: and she must sit in such manner, that she may easily put up her hand (being first annointed) into those parts, when need requires. And by this meanes, she may know, whether the child come naturally, or no, for in feeling gently crosse the membrane, that containes the waters, she shall find, either the roundnesse of the childs head, or else some unevennesse. If in feeling, she perceive that there is any hard and equall roundnesse; it is most likely to be the childs head, and that he comes naturally: but if she feele any unevennesse, the contrarie may be imagined.

When she perceiveth, that all comes well, and according to nature, the throwes increasing upon the woman, and that the child doth strive and endevour to come forth, and the wombe doth straine it selfe to be freed of this burthen; Then the Midwife must incourage the woman, entreating her to hold in her breath, by stopping her mouth, and to straine downward, as though she would go to the stoole: Assuring her, that she shall be quickly eased of her paine: and that her child is even ready to come into the world, exhorting her to be patient, and promising, that she shall have, either a goodly sonne, or a faire daughter, according as she knoweth her affection inclined.

And the Midwives greatest charge must be, that she doe nothing hastily, or rashly, or by force, to inlarge the passage of the child: and much lesse, to let foorth the water, or to breake, and teare the membranes, that containe it: but she must expect till it breake of it selfe.

Some Midwives either through ignorance, or impatience, or else by being hastned to go to some other womans labour, do teare the membranes with their nayles, and let foorth the water, to the great hurt and danger, both of the poore woman, and her child: who remaines drie, the water being issued, and voided before the appointed time; yea, oftentimes before the child be well turned, which hath been the death of many women, and children. But when the water, both by the indevour of the Mother, and likewise of the child, shall be newly broken; then aswell the Midwife, as the rest of the women present, must more and more incourage the woman, especially when her throwes increase; beseeching her in the name of God, that she would farther them, as much as she can possibly. In the meane time, the Midwife must continually annoint the neather parts with butter, or some other fats. And when the head doth offer it selfe to come foorth, she must receive it gently with both her hands: which being come foorth, and the womans throwes increasing, she must draw out the shoulders handsomely, sliding downe her finger under the childs arme-pits; taking the oportunitie and time when her throwes come fastest. And it is to be noted, that the throwes cease verie little, or not at all, after the head and shoulders be once come forth: Never-thelesse, it will be very fit, to give the poore woman a little breathing, intreating her, that she would be of as good cheare as she can. After this, the Midwive having drawen out the shoulders, may easily draw forth the rest of the body: which must not be done either hastily or rashly.

But because the child naturally doth come into the world, with the face downward: therefore when he is quite taken foorth, he must be turned upon his backe: for feare lest hee be stifled, or chok't. And if his navell-string be woond about his necke, (as many times it happens) then must it be unwoond. Oftentimes likewise, the child is so feeble, and faint, that there can scarsely be perceived any breath, or life in him: and therefore he must have a little wine spirted into his mouth, nose, and eares, in that quantitie as shall be needfull. When he is come to himselfe, and begins to crie, then the Midwive must follow the string, wagging and shaking it, thereby to draw, and bring foorth gently the after-birth, to which it is tyed: bidding the woman to cough, and likewise to hold some salt in her hands, fast shut together, and then blow in them.

In the meane time the Midwife, or some other woman, must presse gently with her hand, the top of the womans belly, stroking it lightly downward: the after-burthen being come, it must be laid upon the childs belly: and the child, together with the after-birth, must be wrapp'd up handsomely in a bed, and a blanket, to be carried nearer the fire, covering the head with a linnen cloth five or sixe times double: and yet not exposing him sodainly either to the fire-light, day-light, or candle-light, lest by this sodaine change his sight might be hurt: but his eies must be covered, that by little and little he may open them, and acquaint them with the light. . . .

THE THIRD TIME THAT MUST BE OBSERVED
BY THE MIDWIVE.

As soone as the child is borne, and that the Mother is delivered of her after-birth, the Midwife shall cause her legs to be gently laid downe, taking away the peece of wood, that lay at her feet: and put a fine linnen cloth, or rather a cleane spunge, washed in warme water, and wrung out, betweene her thigh's, neare unto her naturall parts, that the cold ayre may not get therein: and then must she take the

child, together with the after-burthen, and carrie them to the fire, as
hath been said already.

And if it happen, that the after-burthen be long ere it come, or be
drawen foorth; and that the child may not stay so long there, for
danger to be stifled, and die, it being oftentimes verie weake. The
midwive shall first tye, and then cut the childs Navel-string, to
seperat him from the after-burthen: Which must be done in this manner.

She must have in readynesse, a good double thread, and a paire of
sharpe Scissors: with the thread she must tye the Navell a good inch
from the childs belly with a double knot, or ostner; this knot must be
neither too hard and straite, neither too loose: for too straite tying,
beside the extreame paine it causeth, makes that which is tyed fall off
too soone, and that, before the scar be growen betweene the live and
the dead part: And if it be tyed too loose, thereof proceeds a fluxe of
bloud from the umbilicall vessels, which are not exactly closed and
stopp't by the said ligature: and therefore, a meane must be observed
in doing it. Then being thus tyed, the Navel-string must be cut off an
inch beneath the knot; And that the knot may not slip, nor the thred
slide away; she must take a little fine linnen rowler dip't in oile of
Roses, wherewith she must wrap the rest of the Navell, and with a
little fine bumbast moistened in the same oyle, she must lay it upon
the belly, that it be not crusht, when they dresse and swath the child.
By this ligature, that which is tyed will come to wither, and drie of it
selfe, and some foure or five daies after, more, or lesse, the dead part
will fall from the quicke, which must not be forc'd or pluckt off in
any case.

Some do observe, that the Navell must by tyed longer, or shorter,
according to the difference of the sexe, allowing more measure to the
males: because this length doth make their tongue, and privie mem-
bres the longer: whereby they may both speake the plainer, and be
more serviceable to Ladies. And that by tying it short, and almost
close to the belly in females, their tongue is less free, and their
naturall part more straite: And to speake the truth, the Gossips commonly say merrily to the Midwife; if it be a boy, *Make him good
measure*; but if it be a wench, *Tye it short*.

Hippocrates would have them, in tying the Navell, observe this
that followeth. If a woman (saith he) be delivered with paine, and the
child stay long in the wombe, and comes not foorth easily, but with
trouble: and chiefly if it be by the Chirurgians help, and instruments:

such children are not long lived, and therefore there Navell-string must not be cut, before they have either sneez'd, piss'd, or cried.

Anone after the Midwife hath cut the Navell, she must wipe and make clean the child, not onely his face, but his whole bodie, and the wrinkles and folds of the arme-pits, buttocks, and joints, either with fresh Butter, or oyle of sweet Almonds. Some do it with oyle of Roses, others with oyle of Nuts, thereby to make the skin more firme, and to stop the pores, that the outward ayre may not hurt him, and likewise to strengthen all his parts.

Avicen boyleth Roses and Sage in wine, and washeth the child with a fine soft Spung dipt therein: and so continues it three or foure mornings when he is shifted.

The child being thus shifted and annoynted, and then well dried, and wrap't up by the Midwife, or others: they must presently give him a little wine and Suger in a spoone, or else the bignesse of a pease, of *Mithridate*, or *Triacle*, dissolved in a little wine, if it be Winter, and in Summer (by reason of the heat) with a little *Carduus Benedictus*, or some other *Cordiall water*.

Avicen doth thinke it sufficient to give them a little Hony: and to rub the top and bottome of the tongue with ones finger dip't in hony. And by this meanes, to see whether they be tongue tyed, and so to cut the string, if it be needfull.

Ebenezer Parkman (1703-1782), the first minister of Westborough, Massachusetts for 58 years, was the eleventh child of a Boston shipwright. He graduated from Harvard in 1721, married in 1724, and a year later had the first of sixteen children. His rich diary, which reflects the daily life of an ordinary country parson, has been published in the Proceedings *of the American Antiquarian Society. The following passages can be found under the appropriate dates in Volume 71 (1961), pp. 93-227, 361-448, and Volume 72 (1962), pp. 31-233, 329-481.*

September. My Mother rode up with me to Westboro.
1725: 14 September. This Morning was very Cloudy, Not only abroad as to the weather but in the house with respect to my wife who for about Three hours was in great Extremity. I thought I had not been earnest enough with God yet, notwithstanding what passt last night, etc. Then again Engaged in a Short but fervent Devotion,

and Ten Minutes past Eight my wife was delivered of a Daughter. I cryed unto God most high, unto God who is a very present Help in time of Trouble and performeth all things for us, and He brought Salvation. He put joy and Gladness into our Hearts; and O that we may never forget his Benefits!

17 September. My Father came up to us.

19 September. The Child was Solemnly given up to God in Baptism (My Father holding it up). I call'd it (by my wife's Name) Mary.

28 September. My Father and Mother rode to Boston. My mother stopt at Marlboro being ill.

4 October. Mother Champney [his wife's mother] came up, being brought up by Father Champney.

My wife a very Sore Breast.

Breast Broke under Mrs. Whitcombs Care.

Breast Broke a Second Time.

8 November. I rode down with Mother Champney to Cambridge.

15 November. I was call'd out to see Mrs. Tomlin who was in Travail [labor] and in terrible Fits. She continued in them in a very awfull and Ghastly manner. The Infant was Dead at the Birth.

16 November. Mrs. Tomlin dy'd, a Sore Trial to the Young Man, Who in such a mann'r Lost his First wife and Child.

1726: 10 July. I preach'd all Day upon Jer. 4, 14. My Wife was Taken with a shivering and Trembling while in the afternoon Exercise, but Showed nothing to me till I was come out of meeting, when She walked very Slow and look'd more pale and sunk than I had ever seen her on any occasion that I remember. But she made a shift to get home and then grew somewhat better. I concluded it to be issue proceeding from the Procidantia Uteri which she had been Troubled with. This accident put us upon Weaning the Child which this Night began.

16 July. We were very low at the news my wife being oppress'd with Every illness: The Procidantia, etc., the turning of her Milk, Her Mouth Obstructed, pain in her Breast, and great pain and weakness in Every part.

17 July. My Wive rose out of Bed but exceeding ill, bound together with her Excessive pains; came down; I'm afraid took Some Air at the Door; grew much worse. I got her up Stairs in order to go to Bed again, but she almost swoon'd away. Recovering a little from her faintings, She demonstrated to us that she was in grievous ago-

nies. She undress'd and with the Tenderest Help [of] her Mother and myself She was assisted to Bed. But Every maladie was Enraged, by Every weakness and discouragement left almost Lifeless. I walked a little in the Room, her mother holding in one hand her hand, her other laid upon her Head. I cast my Eyes now and then upon her and Concluded she was drowsing, but I went to her to look upon her, and Spoke to her. Receiving no kind of Return Her Mother put her hand to her mouth. I urg'd Some Testification or sign, but none being given; but she lay in a profound stillness when as tho had hitherto been vigorously strugling Her Teeth were set, her Limbs Cold, her Eyes Distorted, and very Little Life any where perceptible, when her Mother gave me the word that She was Dying. How I felt ougoes Description. I hastened the Maid to Mrs. Forbush. My Wife Lay for the space of 3 quarters of or altogether an hour I suppose in such a Condition. O Dismal Hour, wherein the Struggle with my heart for her Division was like the Rending the Soul from the Body! It was truly a most gloomy Time! Mrs. Forbush came just when She spoke, a Galbunum Plaister was taken off which was too strong for her. Something was given her and She Revid'd a little but Continued in the Last Extremitys. It was a Reprieve but it Seem'd a Short one. We Expected we must be Rent asunder this Day! It grew more and more Intollerable! I was full of prayers and anon I had Some Hope. I grew more Confirmed in Hope. It brought fresh to my Mind all the Bitter Sufferings of her Dark friday, Ever long, about nine Months before, wherein I had the Same prospects. The Salvations of God then, strengthened my Trust in him. She became more sensible. We Encouraged ourselves in the Lord and He show'd us his Mercy. While We have any being let us praise the Lord!

31 August. My Child not well, she now breading her Eye Teeth.

8 September. We Sent to Dr. Matthews for Little Molly [Mary] ill with a fever and violent flux. The cause was from her breading her Eye Teeth. We have Sometimes been up with her till after midnight. My wive has not had a Comfortable night's Rest this week. I reflected upon Davids case when his Child was Sick.

9 September. My Babe I hope is better and in some method of Recovery.

5 December. Mr. Thomas Forbush, Junior's youngest Child dy'd very suddenly this morning, as I hear many Young Children in severall Towns round here. In the Eve my Little Dauter was ill, But

6 December. Thro the Divine Favour She was this Morning well recovered. In the Afternoon I was at the funerall of Mr. Forbush's Child.

1727: 19 August. In the Afternoon my wife was pained, but no great Complaint till the Evening when She grew very ill. I went to Bed Somewhat late but could lie but a very few minutes. I rose and (being, as I gathered about midnight) rode to Mrs. Forbush and brought her up But she was not very much Employ'd till morning.

20 August. I rode for Mrs. Byles and sent for other neighbouring women. My wife had many pains, But I Saw Liberty to go to Meeting at the proper hour. I delivered the morning Sermon upon I Chron. 28, 9. In the Afternoon I preach'd upon Rom. 11, 36 wherein I had occasion to Mention the Kings Death, and to give fair hints at the Circumstances of my Family. When I came home at Even my wive was Still full of pains but no imediate apprehension that she should be delivered. But, a little more than half an hour after sunset (having been no long time in Extremity) She was Delivered, and the will of God was to favour me in a very high Degree. God gave Me a Son, which I have set up for my Ebenezer, for hitherto the Lord hath Helped Me. We have indeed a great deal of Reason to praise and magnifie the name of our gracious God who So Signally and mercifully appears for us, and lays us under ten thousand the strongest obligations to him. O that I may never forget his Benefits! But O that I may both Live and Speak Gods praises! Were comfortably carry'd thro the night. Blessed be God!

24 August. My Wive and Infant through the Divine Goodness in very hopefull and favourable Circumstances. Little or nothing that was difficult with us.

26 August. If on Saturdayes in Generall I am professedly more employ'd than on any other Dayes I am Surely to be thought to be more on this, and I Endeavoured to possess my Thoughts in all Seriousness, of the Weighty and Solemn Transaction of Dedicating my Son to God, and I would in the Fear of God Undertake this Sacred Business.

27 August. I Sincerely comitted the great Article of offering my Son unto God and implor'd the divine direction and assistance, with Confession of my Sins and Thankfull acknowledgements of all especially his Signal Mercies. I then proceeded to the Exercises of the Day, and preach'd in the Morning on Mat. 19, 13, 14, 15, as I did in the afternoon likewise on the Same. And then (I hope in the integrity

of my Heart and with Souls Desire of the Glory of God and the invaluable Spirituall Blessings of the Covenant) I baptiz'd My Son Ebenezer and put him into the Arms of the Savior that He might Bless Him according to the gracious Encouragement given to His People. And I hope I found Favours with the Lord. Mr. Joseph Wheeler presented His Son Aaron at the Same time. The Lord has done great things for me for which I was filled with Joy and Gladness. O that Gods Grace may be given me that I may alwayes walk in a suitable manner Before Him. At this Season I improv'd the Opportunity [to] renew the Dedication of my Self and My Dauter Mary and all mine unto our glorious God in the Covenant of Grace.

1738: 20 February. My wife [Hannah Breck, 22; his wife Mary died 29 January 1736] had a very ill turn, and had been very ill for Two Dayes. Keeps her Chamber. Abort, etc., etc. [miscarriage]

16 December. My wife has not only Swell'd greatly in her Limbs but (besides her pregnancy) in her Body, and is exceeding full of Pain. I sent Ebenezer [his first son] to Marlborough to the Doctor's.

26 December. A little after 4 in the morning my Wife call'd Me up by her extreme pains prevailing upon her and changing into signs of Travail. I rode over to Deacon Forbush's and brought her [Mrs. Forbush] over as our midwife. Sister Hicks, old Mrs. Knowlton, Mrs. Whipple, Mrs. Hephzibath Maynard, Mrs. Byles and Mrs. Rogers were call'd and brought and stay'd all Day and Night.

27 December. In the morning the Women Scattered away to their several Homes except Mrs. Forbush who did not leave us.

28 December. At about 4 in the morning Mrs. Forbush call'd me up with great earnestness to gather some women together. It was very Cold, and I ran on foot to sister Hicks and to old Mrs. Knowlton— sent to Mrs. Maynard and rode to Mrs. Byles, all which came together by Daybreak. We were in the Article of Distress. About Seven o'Clock my Fourth Daughter was born. An exceeding Small Child and great doubt whether it would continue alive. But my wife in a good State, through the wondrous Goodness and Mercy of God. A Cold Day. Sent Ebenezer Maynard to Dr. Gotts, and to call Mrs. Mary Sherman to Nurse. Nurse watch'd.

30 December. My wive in great Pain. Mrs. Maynard here. At Evening my wife exceedingly pained under her Breasts—thought to be the Coming of her milk. Molly Lee and the Nurse watch'd.

31 December. My Wive easier to Day. Rebecca Hicks watch'd.

1739: 4 January. My Wife makes no great Haste in Recovery, but the Child is very weak and feeble yet, and the sore Mouth has been prevailing upon it for some time. Abiel Allen watch'd. Cold Season.

5 January. My Wife very faint and weak, fainting in going from the bed to the Table. Ruth Hicks watch'd. Cold continues. Boys sled wood.

6 January. My Wife feeble. Childs Sore mouth continues Bad. Rebecca watch'd.

7 January. Moderate fine Day. At Eve Rebecca Taynter tarried and watch'd. My wife somewhat more Comfortable. The Child in doubtfull State by its Sore Mouth. N.B. Publick Prayers for the Child.

8 January. Old Mrs. Knowlton and Mrs. Maynard here. Boys cutting wood within the Fence. Child very bad. Mrs. Maynard watch'd.

9 January. The Child extreme bad, especially the latter part of the Day. Boys sledded home wood. P.M. and Evening we thought the Child was dying—took nothing for many Hours, a Ghastly pale overspread the Visage and appear'd choak'd up; sometimes was Seemingly gone for some while together. We pray'd for it p.m. All night distress'd about it and expecting its last Gasp. Nurse and my Dauter Molly sat up with it.

10 January. Through the Great Mercy of God the Child is alive this morning—and Continues—the sore mouth abates—peels and clears off.

11 January. Frequent Snows. Trees ever so loaded yesterday when I rode over to the North side of the Town that it was very difficult passing, It being very deep in the Roads, yet it Snow'd again to Day. The Child somewhat better. Martha Maynard Watch'd. Storm continues.

12 January. A very great Storm, Windy, Cold and Snow'd very fast. Nurse Watch'd.

13 January. Sent for to visit Captain Warrin's Wife who was deliver'd of a very large Child this morning, but herself in a very low distressing Condition. Abiel watch'd.

14 January. A Morning of great Trouble! The Childs soreness of Mouth had return'd for Two or Three Days, but we did not judge it in immediate Danger. There was nothing of this discover'd in the first of the Morning. But about nine o'Clock I was call'd down from my Study with the Alarm that the Child was dying! About 10 She ceas'd to breath! The will of the Lord be done! I preach'd on Rev. 20, 12. O that we might have a due sense of the Divine Mind Concerning us!

15 January. Deacon Newton kindly came and brought Two Bottles of wine and offer'd to go to Marlborough upon what Errands would be Necessary to be done there. Ensign Maynard went to Mr. Cushings. Ebenezer Maynard dugg the Grave. The Snow exceeding Deep, by which means it was very difficult to break away to get wood, for 3 Fires and one so long all night as well as Day, had wasted wood at a very great Rate. Yet we got a Supply.

16 January. Mr. Cushing and his Wive came to the Funeral of my Infant Elizabeth. The Weather was moderate. The Neighbours in very considerable Numbers, attended. I desire to interr my Dead in the Faith of the new Covenant and of the glorious Privilege of the Ressurection to Eternal Life. N.B. Nurse was bearer. No Friends from Marlborough. N.B. Mr. Cushing and his Wife could not go to the Grave.

17 January. My wife was exceeding full of pain.

18 January. My wife easier this morning, but very weak.

19 January. My Wife exceeding full of pain again, weak and distress'd, her lower Limbs grow useless and one of her feet swells again.

22 January. My Wife very full of Pain yet!

25 January. My [wife] has not been easy ever since the 17th Day.

27 January. My Wife Easyer and Stronger, but I was not very well.

31 January. My Wife lys ill yet, but gathers Some Strength and can begin to take a step or Two with Help.

5 February. Mr. Samuel Fay juniors Infant Child bury'd which bled to Death at the Navel. My wive grows worse, her pains being Sharper for the Time than with the former Legg.

14 February. My Wife somewhat better.

17 February. My Wife grows Still better. Nurse went home having been with us full seven Weeks.

25 February. N.B. My Wife walk'd across the room, a thing she has not done these Three weeks, and she din'd with us to Day.

25 December. My Wife had been not well in the Night—continued ill at Times with Travail pains most of the Day, yet kept up, and din'd with us. I sent for Mrs. Clark of Shrewsbury but she was not at Home. I sent for Mrs. Forbush and she came. Sister Hicks also was sent for and her Husband with her again about 10 o'Clock at Night to get us more help. About 12 (although she had gone but about 5 Months) She was deliver'd of a tender, lifeless, Male Child, The Measure of which was 13-1/2 Inches long. Immature for Birth, Yet

with all its parts perfect. But my wife through the great Goodness and Mercy of God in an hopefull State.

26 December. a Snowy Day. I improv'd Ebenezer Maynard to Digg a Grave for the Stillborn, little Babe and Brother Hicks made a Coffin, but did not Colour it. Mrs. Forbush tarried with us. The Deacon came in the Evening, and we improv'd him to bury the Infant.

28 December. Mrs. Forbush called up out of her Bed and carry'd off by Neighbour [Joseph] Thurston, But my Wife in a fine way—had got up to Day.

1740: 10 October. Last Night my Wife had a terrible Convulsion Fitt, But through Gods great mercy it did not continue long. She by Degrees came to her Senses again. Brother Hicks was call'd and sent for Dr. Gott. His young man came, he being himself at Boston, celebrating his own Nuptials. The young man attempted to Bleed my Wife but miss'd the Veins Some Number of Times; but when daily Light came on he succeeded and she bled freely. She was in her pregnancy 4 or 5 Months gone. The bleeding She judg'd was very beneficial to her.

1744: 12 July. My Wife not well. Last night we began to Wean Sarah [born 20 March 1743].

13 July. N.B. The Child weans without Trouble.

1745: 13 March. A Storm of Snow. My Wife gave us the Alarm. I hasted to old Mr. Maynards and got Nathan to go for Mrs. Forbush, who was brought. Nathan went also for Divers other Women. We got as many together as were needed, before or by 12 o'Clock. By Gods Power and Mercy my wife was deliver'd of her Third but my Sixth Daughter, being my Ninth Living Child about 1/2 past 2 o'Clock. The Glory be to God! May We who are the Instruments of its Natural be under God, of its Spiritual Birth! And may the Lord yet magnifie his Mercy to His Handmaid and recover her to Health and Strength again! Nor We be unmindfull of God's Goodness or our Obligations to Him therefor! The Women assisting to Mrs. Forbush were the following—viz. old Mrs. Whipple, Mrs. Rogers, Mrs. Maynard, Mrs. How, Captain Samuel Forbushs and Lieutenant Aaron Forbush Wife's. Our Eating was over before Night—prayer also—and Thomme [his second son] began to carry Home the Women, tho some of them tarry'd in the Evening whilst others were returning. But Granny Forbush tarry'd all Night.

17 March. A.M. Preparatory to the Solemnity of Dedicating my

young Child I preach'd on Ps. 51, 15 and p.m. on Gen. 17, 7. It was baptized by the Name of Susanna. God grant his Covenant may be with me and mine.

While he was minister of the Roxbury, Massachusetts, church, John Eliot (1604-1690), the famous missionary to the Indians, kept a memoir of church affairs that sheds light on the trials of childbirth in the first century of colonial New England. The following excerpts are taken from the Roxbury Land and Church Records published in the sixth volume of the Report *of the* [Boston] Record Commissioners *(Boston, 2nd ed. 1884), pp. 170-207.*

1642: November. There were 2 infants dyed in the birth, it was conceived to be through the unskilfullnesse of the midwife, none of the p[ar]ents were of o[u]r church.

1643: 4 April. Mary Onion the wife of Rob. Onion died of a cold and sweat taken in childbed; her child also dyed, because she was stubborne, and would not submitt to the paines, but she was after filled with dredful horror of conscience and dyed under them, but I hope und[e]r some tokens of mercy.

1647: 7 October. Goodwife Turner dyed in child bed, a godly young woman, though not yet admitted [to the church], yet should had not her travail [labor] pr[e]vented.

1648: 23 January. Sarah Davis, bro. Morel's daughter dyed, by ocasion of unheedfull taking cold upon an abortion [miscarriage].

1649: 8 November. Sister Heli dyed in childbed w[i]th oth[e]r diseases wh[ich] cause[d] her child to dy & was taken fro[m] her by peeches [forceps].

1667-68: This winter many women died in childbirth not being able to be delivered, as [Rebecca] Craft, Alice Davis, in our Town, and severall in other Towns.

1678: 11 February. A new borne infant of Robert Peirpont dyed by falling out of [the] lap of a girle th[a]t had it & slep[t], so leting it fall.

1679: 4 July. Mary, the daughter of Caleb Lamb, she dyed of the pox. The eyes of the child w[e]r[e] forced out of the head by the v[i]olence of the disease.

Baptism records:

1644: 5 May. Peniel Bowen . . . [his father] living at a farme neerer to us then to Boston, his wife was delivered of this child by Gods mercy w[i]thout the help of any oth[e]r woman. God himself helping his pore servants in a straight.

1605: 15 September. Joseph Weld, son of John Weld. There was no help present w[he]n the mother was delivered of this child.

From literary sources—such as diaries and church records—it is easy to get the impression that infant mortality in colonial New England was extremely high. The only way to verify that impression is to count *all* the children born in a given town over time and *all* the deaths at various ages. This can be done from the records of births, deaths, and marriages kept by the town clerks of all New England towns since the early 17th century. Philip Greven has carefully calculated the vital statistics of one such town in *Four Generations: Population, Land, and Family in Colonial Andover, Massachusetts* (Ithaca, 1970). The following tables are derived from his more detailed tables found on pp. 189 and 191 of that book. Note that demographical statistics are given per thousand, not in percentages; if you are more comfortable with percentages, point off one decimal to the left in the figures in the right-hand columns.

Table 1. Mortality rate for persons born in Andover, Massachusetts between 1670 and 1759 and dying before age 20.

| Birth group and age at death | Deaths | | | Birth group members (d.) | Mortality rate |
	(a) Male	(b) Female	(c) Total		c/ 1000d
1670-1699					
0-1 years	37	22	59	512	115
2-9 years	12	3	15	453	33
10-19 years	15	8	13	438	30
Total, 0-19 years	54	33	87	512	170
1700-1729					
0-1 years	77	50	127	838	152
2-9 years	18	18	36	711	51
10-19 years	17	26	43	675	64
Total, 0-19 years	112	94	206	838	246
1730-1759					
0-1 years	45	21	66	423	156
2-9 years	33	30	63	357	176
10-19 years	6	7	13	294	44
Total, 0-19 years	84	58	142	423	336

Table 2. Rate of survival to age 10 for children born in Andover, Massachusetts between 1640 and 1759.

Birth group	Birth group members (a)	Probable survivors (b)	Survival rate b/ 1000a
1640-1669	204	187	917
1670-1699	512	438	855
1700-1729	838	675	805
1730-1759	423	294	695

II. GROWTH

The growing child is a learning child and therefore adventurous. As soon as the total dependence of the cradle is passed, the child begins to learn the ways of independence and adulthood. Why was childhood so dangerous, according to Puritan adults? What was the source of these dangers? Who was responsible for removing them? In what ways did Puritan society try to remove them? Do you think that this was an easy task for most parents? How did Puritan parents regard their children? Did mothers regard them any differently than fathers? Why? What effect do you think Puritan upbringing had on the children themselves? What kind of children were they? What kind of adults? How can you tell? What other kinds of evidence would tell you about the kind of children they were? Was formal education important to the Puritans? Why? What are some of the ways you can tell? Are schools different today? Are they similar? What has happened in the past two hundred years that might explain this?

One of the rarest and most intimate glimpses of the growing child in New England is provided by the journal-letters of Esther Burr (1732-58), daughter of Jonathan Edwards of Stockbridge, Massachusetts, the most powerful minister in colonial New England, and wife of Aaron Burr (1715-57), a Presbyterian minister and the second president of Princeton. Although they were written from New Jersey where she and her family had recently moved, her letters to a young friend, Sarah Prince, in Boston reflect her own New England upbringing and the shared knowledge of her New England friend. These unique letters are in the Beinecke Library of Yale University and have not been published.

1754: 1 October. In the Morn Sally [her daughter] awakes me with her prattle, like *other Birds*, as soon as she is awake to Singing . . . the first thing after her Eyes are open is to look for me & as soon as she sees me a very pleasant smile her Eyes sparkling like *diamonds*. She is very good company when I have no other.

5 November. In the Morn I rise e[a]rly my first business is to dress *Sally*, for I dont love to see Children naked till Noon.

November, Friday. You my dear cant immagine how much pleased of late Mr Burr is with his little Daughter, he begins to think she is good to kiss, & thinks he sees a great many beauties in her, that he used to be perfectly blind to, he complains she is another temptation to him, to spend two much time with her—he does love to play with her dearly.

1755: 28 February, Friday. I had almost forgot to tell you that I have begun to govourn Sally. She has been whip'd once on *Old Adams* account, & she knows the differance between a Smile & a frown as well as I do, when she has done any thing that she suspects is wrong, will look with concern to see what Mamma says, & if I only knit my brow she will cry till I smile, and altho' she is not quite Ten months old, yet when she knows so much, I think tis time she should be taught. But none but a parent can conceive how hard it is to chastise your *own most tender self*. I confess I never had a right idea of the mothers heart at such a time before, I did it my self two, & I did her a vast deal of good. If you was here I would tell you the effect it had on her.

March, Thursday. Tis very strange that I should forget to tell you that this day Sally began to speak so as to be understood. She trys to say Mamma & very pret[t]ely brings out Mam—which is above half the word.

March, Thursday. I find I was not settled till I had a Child, & now I am effectually settled, a Journey seems a Vast thing. I am to go to Princeton soon [from their home in Elizabethtown], which seems like Ansons voyage almost.

7 April. Sally recovers [from a serious illness which brought her near death] . . . but is very cross. I am affraid this illness will cost [her] a whiping Spel.

20 April. [Sally near death again.] She has been extreamly tendsome, would go to no Stranger, so Sukey [a young maid servant] & I have been obliged to watch every Night ever since her sickness that I am almost got to be as bad as the Child. [Letter written at]

Two O'Clock in the Night as Sally is a Sleep in the Cradle & I a rocking.

23 April. [Sally much improved but] is extreamly cross, crying all day *Mam—Mam* if I hant her in my Arms, that she is more troublesom than when she was sicker altho' tis not so distressing.

June. I ha'nt told you that Sally runs alone. She began to walk the day she was 14 months old. She is backward with her feet, tho she has walked by things all over the house almost 4 months, but now she does go. She does very well, she will go out doors or any where.

14 July. We have lately discovered that Sallys Neck is crooked, her Head grows leaning upon her right Sholder, whether it is natural or come by habit we cant tell but so it is . . . Mr Burr seems much distressed about it, I think more than I am, what to do we know not, but Mr Burr thinks to go into New England to one Doct. Porter at Wethersfield [Connecticut] who is the most skilfull Surgeon in this part of the World perhaps—but what is best God only knows, he has wise ends in view no doubt, perhaps He fore-saw that we should be two Proud of her, & so has sent this calamaty to mortify us & her—Mr Burr says if she was a Boy he should [not] much care about it, but I am not sertain but he would be more concernd about it, for it does make a Man look underling & meaching.

23 July. I must tell you some of Sallys witt—Miss Sukey shews her the picture of a Face that was Black, & tells her it was a Baby, she must Buss it, & she almost got her mouth to it, when she started back & said it was Nanny (for so she calls Harry [their Negro kitchen helper]) &   would not Buss it, nor have any thing to do with it.

3 August. [Shortly after hearing news of General Braddock's defeat by the French and Indians in neighboring Pennsylvania] You cant conceive my dear friend what a tender Mother under goes for her children at such a day as this, to think of bring[ing] up Children to be *dashed against the Stones by our barbarous enemies*—or which is worse, to be inslaved by them, & obliged to turn *Papist*—it seems to me some times if I had no Child nor was likely to have any that I should not be much distressed, but I must leve the subject tis two dreadfull to think off.

30 October. [After she was very ill with worms, for which she was purged and vomitted,] Now Sally is better I begin to feel that I am almost worried out for she will go to nobody but me.

31 October. Sally has got upon her feet again, & could get out of my lap & run to her Papa, & make her honours & *say papa* & kiss him.

5 November. [News that bands of French and Indians are marauding the backcountries of the southern provinces, even to the New Jersey borders.] Unless the God of Armies undertakes for us we are lost, for our people seem to know nothing what to do nor more than a parsle of Children would in such a case, nor half so much as New-England Children would.

11 November. *Most Sho[c]king news*—That 17 men of War are Landed in Cabritton—I see nothing but *distruction* before us—*Universal distruction*—And *Wo* to them that are *with Child*, to them that give Suck in these days!

29 December. [Governor Belcher, his wife, and others came to visit.] Sally to be sure must make Sport for us, Mad[a]m [Belcher] could not perswade her to go to her or say anything to her, but the Shit [?] would go to Justice Belcher [the Governor's son] & kiss him—I was almost vexed with her.

1756: 6 February. [Aaron Burr was born, Sally's brother and the future Vice-President of the United States.]

13 April. When I had but one Child my hands were tied, but now I am tied hand & foot (how I shall get along when I have got 1/2 dzn. or 10 Children I cant devise). I have no help in the House except what is in our Kitchen & you know what that is [Harry, the Negro].

14 April. P.S. As I stept out of the Room Miss Sally gets this & has rumpled it that tis not fit to send—but you will excuse it—I scolded at her but she said she was ageing to write.

16 April. P.S. Now my zeal is a little cold I feel as I do after whiping Sally prety hard &am afraid I have whiped her more then was needfull . . . Sally can Speak quite plain & Little Aaron begins to smile & play; he is a fine quiet Child.

19 April. [Mr. Burr leaves on a trip to Boston.] Little Sally observing my gloom upon Mr Burrs leveing me set her self very pretily on & think[s] to comfort me. She immagined I was sick—She says *MammapoorMammaisSick—dontbeSickMamma—Papaantgone*—upon this I Smiled, the little cretur's Eyes Sparkled for Joy & she says . . .*Mamma ant Sick—dear Mamma* &c. Theirs a Mother for you.

May. The Buttons I timidly thank you for & have put em into Sallys Sleves as you desire—Sally says in her Language—*O-Mit Pint give Tally fine Buttons, that a Dood Mit Pint, Tally love Mit Pint*— Now I must interpret it or you will never find it out—O Miss Prince give Sally fine Buttons, that a good Miss Prince, Sally love Miss Prince.

29 October. [On Sarah Prince's proposed marriage to a man with children by his first marriage.] As to the first objection you make I think it rather an Inducement tis best they should be Boys; they wont make you half the trouble that Girls might. Be sure if you should have Children of your own—Boys want the same principles of relegion & Virtue instilled into them as Girls, & I cant see why you hant an oppertunity of doing as much good, as they are young you will have quite the assendent over them.

1757: 2 September. [After a bout of the throat distemper and worms] Sally has got prety hearty again, is not much of a Baby, affects to be thought a Woman, nothing she scorns more then to be told she is a Baby or Child. We are about sending her to School, but Mr Burr is expecting that she will prove a Numbhead, but for my part I think her about Middling on all accounts—She grows thinner & more shapeable. I have taken her to Meeting & she behaves very well & can give a good account [of] what Papa does there—She can say some of Doct. Watts verses by heart & the Lords prayer & some other prayers, but she is not over apt about the matter. Aaron is a little dirty Noisy Boy very different from Sally almost in every thing. He begins to talk a little, is very Sly & Mischevious. He has more Sprightliness then Sally & must say he is handsomer, but not so good Tempered. He is very resolute & requires a good Governor to bring him to terms.

The serious Puritan concern for the spiritual welfare of children shows through the sober essay of John Robinson (1575-1625), the leading religious light of the Plymouth Colony. A graduate of Cambridge University, he moved to Leyden in Holland in 1608 to minister to the Pilgrim congregation there but died in 1625 before he could join them in America. The following essay on "Children" appears in The Works of John Robinson, *ed. Robert Ashton (Boston, 1851), vol. 1, pp. 244-250.*

Children, in their first days, have the greater benefit of good mothers, not only because they suck their milk, but in a sort, their manners also, by being continually with them, and receiving their first impressions from them. But afterwards, when they come to riper years, good fathers are more behoveful for their forming in virtue and good manners, by their greater wisdom and authority: and ofttimes also, by correcting the fruits of their mother's indulgence, by their severity.

They are a blessing great, but dangerous. They come into the world at first with danger, both in respect of themselves, as passing sometimes, from the womb to the grave; sometimes, being born deformed in body; sometimes, incapable of understanding: as also in regard of the mother, the first day of their being in the world, being often her last in it. After their coming into the world through so many dangers, they come even into a world of dangers. In their infancy, how soon is the tender bud nipped, or bruised by sickness or otherwise! In their ventursome days, into how many needless dangers do they throw themselves, in which many perish, besides those into which God brings them, and that all their life long! Above all other, how great and many are their spiritual dangers, both for nourishing and increasing the corruption which they bring into the world with them; and for diverting them from all goodness, which God's grace, and men's endeavour might work in them! These dangers and difficulties, howsoever they make not God's blessings in giving children to be no blessings, or deserving to be lightly esteemed; yet should they moderate our desire of them, and grief for their want: that none should say either to God or one to another, as Rachel did to Jacob, "Give me children, or else I die," Gen. XXX. 1: specially if we weigh withal, that though the Lord give us divers towardly, and good; yet one or two proving lewd and wicked will break our tender hearts, more than all the rest will comfort us: like as in the natural body there is more grief by the aching of some one part, though but a tooth, than comfort and ease in the good and sound state of all the rest. If children considered aright of the careful thoughts, sorrows and fears, and sore pains withal of their parents, they would think they owed them more honour, service and obedience, than, for the most part, they do. We seldom consider and prize worthily the cares and pains of parents, till we become parents ourselves, and learn them by experience.

Many bodily diseases are hereditary; and so are many spiritual, in a sort; and that both by natural inclination, and moral imitation much more: that, as the Lord saith of Israel, "Thou art thy mother's daughter," Ezek. xvi. 45, so may it be said of many, that they are their fathers' and mothers' sons and daughters in evil. Yet, if it so come to pass, that God vouchsafe grace to the child of a wicked father, and that he see the sins which he hath done, he commonly hates them more vehemently, than if they had been in a stranger; and good reason, considering how they have been his dearest parent's ruin. Yea further, even where grace is wanting, the child, ofttimes, by observing and sometimes by feeling also the evil of his father's sin, is driven, though not from his evil way into a good way, yet into the contrary evil. Thus a covetous father often makes a prodigal son; so doth a prodigal a covetous. The son of the covetous taking knowledge how odious his father's covetousness is to all; and therewith persuading himself, and being persuaded by others about him, that there is enough, and more than enough for him, takes occasion as prodigally to pour out, as his father hath miserly hoarded up: as on the contrary, the son of the prodigal both seeing, and feeling the hurt of his parent's lavishness, is thereby provoked to lay the harder about him, for the repairing of his father's ruins.

Love rather descends, than ascends; as streams of water do; and no marvel, if men love where they live, as parents do in children, and not they in them. Hence also is it, that grandfathers are more affectionate towards their children's children, than to their immediates, as seeing themselves further propagated in them, and by their means proceeding on to a further degree of eternity, which all desire naturally, if not in themselves, yet in their posterity. And hence it is, that children brought up with their grandfathers, or grandmothers, seldom do well, but usually corrupted by their too great indulgence.

It is much controverted, whether it be better, in the general, to bring up children under the severity of discipline, and the rod, or no. And the wisdom of the flesh out of love to its own, alleges many reasons to the contrary. But say men what they will, or can, the wisdom of God is best; and that saith, that "foolishness is bound up in the heart of a child, which the rod of correction must drive out:" and that "he, who spares his rod, hurts his son," Prov. xxii. 15; xiii. 24; not in the affection of person, but effect of thing. And surely there is in all children, though not alike, a stubbornness, and stoutness of mind arising from natural pride, which must, in the first place, be broken and beaten down; that so the foundation of their education being laid in humility and tractableness, other virtues may, in their time, be built thereon. This fruit of natural corruption and root of actual rebellion both against God and man must be destroyed, and no manner of way nourished, except we will plant a nursery of contempt of all good persons and things, and of obstinacy therein. It is commendable in a horse, that he be stout and stomachful, being never to be left to his own government, but always to have his rider on his back, and the bit in his mouth. But who would have his child like his horse in his brutishness? Indeed such as are of great stomach, being thoroughly broken, and informed, become very serviceable, for great designs: else, of horses they become asses, or worse: as Themistocles' master told him, when he was a child, that either he would bring some great good, or some great hurt to the commonwealth. Neither is there need to fear, lest by this breaking, the children of great men should prove base-spirited and abject, and so unapt to great employments: for being Adam's sons, whose desire was to have been like unto God, and having those advantages for masterfulness and high thoughts, which great men's children want not, unto whom great affairs are appropriated usually, they will not easily be found unfurnished of stomach and stoutness of mind more than enough; wherein a little is dangerous, specially for making them unmeet for Christ's yoke, and to learn of him, who was lowly, and meek. Matt. xi. 29.

For the beating, and keeping down of this stubbornness parents must provide carefully for two things: first that children's wills and wilfulness be restrained and repressed, and that, in time; lest sooner than they imagine, the tender sprigs grow to that stiffness, that they will rather break than bow. Children should not know, if it could be kept from them, that they have a will in their own, but in their parents' keeping: neither should these words be heard from them, save by way of consent, "I will" or "I will not." And, if will be suffered at first to sway in them in small and lawful things, they will hardly after be restrained in great and ill matters, which their partial conceit, and inexperienced youth, with the lusts thereof and desire of liberty, shall deem small and lawful, as the former. And though good education, specially the grace of God, may afterwards purge out much other evil and weaken this also: yet will such unbroken youth most commonly draw after it great disquietness in crosses, when they fall; and in the whole course of life, a kind of unwieldiness, inflexibility and obstinacy, prejudicial to the parties themselves and uncomfortable, at least, to such as converse with them. The second help is an inuring of them from the first, to such a meanness in all things, as may rather pluck them down, than lift them up: as by plain, and homely diet, and apparel; sending them to school betimes; and bestowing them afterwards, as they are fit, in some course of life, in which they may be exercised diligently, and the same rather under than above their estate: by not abetting them one against another, nor against any, specially before their faces, without great cause: nor by making them men and women, before they become good boys and girls. How oft have I observed, that parents, who have neither failed in diligent instructing of their children, nor in giving them good example, nor in correcting them duly, have only by straining too high this way, either endangered, or utterly overthrown their posterity! hereby lifting them up in their vain hearts, and teaching them to despise both mean things and persons; and themselves also, many times, amongst others: thereby drowning them, Icarus like, in a sea of mischief and misery, by their flying too high a pitch. And this must be the more minded, because there is in men an inbred desire, and that inordinate usually, to hoist up their children, as high, as may be: so as they half think they do them wrong, if they set them not higher, or as high, at least, as themselves, almost whether God will or no. Yea what place affords not some such, as make themselves their children's slaves, not caring how basely they themselves grovel in the earth, so they may set them on their tiptoes.

But first of all for children's competent education, specially for their disposing in some particular course, on which all are to settle at last, though some liberty of stepping this way, or that be given them for a while; as a man, though for his pleasure he see many places, yet seeks his abode in some one in the end, there is required in their parents a thorough discerning and right judgment of their disposition; which is as difficult, as necessary. The difficulty ariseth from the partiality of parents towards their own: for that as the crow thinks her own bird fairest, so do they commonly their children towardly, and better than they are, or than any other indifferent judge doth. This partiality in many is so gross, as they not only deem small good things in them, great, and great evils, small; but often account the same things well becoming them and commendable, which in others they would censure as indecent, and, it may be, enormous. This pernicious error ariseth from self-love. For, as in nature, the object cannot be seen, which is either too near the eye, or too far from it; so neither can the disposition of that child be rightly discerned, which lieth too near his father's heart. And yet is the knowledge of this, so necessary, that we build not either upon a vain, or uncertain foundation, with great hazard of loss, both of labour, and expense, in sorting our child to his particular calling and course of life; as all without it, is but a very rash adventure. For as none are fit for every course, nor hardly any for many, in any great degree, so every one is fit for one or other: to which if his ability, and disposition be applied, with any convenient diligence on his part and helps by others; he may easily come to a mediocrity therein, if not to some rareness. Hence was it, that fathers in some places, used to lead their children to the shops of all kind of artificers, to try how they could both handle their tools, and like their works; that so they might bestow them accordingly. Some wise men also have wished, that there might be established, by public authority, a course for the due trial, and choice of wits for several sciences. And surely, where there goes not before a natural aptness and moral disposition also for some calling; there will follow nothing but loss: loss of time, loss of labour, loss of charges, and all; as when the seed is cast into the barren ground. And as the midwife how skilful soever in her art, cannot make the woman to be delivered, that was not first with child; so neither can the best masters make their scholars, or servants, to bring forth sciences, unless they have an aptness thereunto first conceived in their brains.

There is running in the breasts of most parents a strong stream of partial affection towards some one, or other of their children, above the rest, either for its beauty or wit or likeness to themselves, or some other fancied good in it; which is always dangerous, and oft hurtful. Sometimes the Lord takes away such before the rest, to punish the father's fondness: and most commonly such if surviving, prove the worst of all the rest, as growing hereby proud, and arrogant in themselves, presumptuous upon their father's love, and contemptuous of the rest of their brethren, and sisters; as we may see in Esau, Absalom, and Adonijah, their fathers' darlings; and in many more, in our daily experience. And though they in themselves, which they seldom are free from, be not corrupted with pride; yet will the rest seldom, or never escape the infection of envy at it; as is to be seen in Joseph's brethren. It is natural for parents tenderly to love all their chldren; and best for them to be as equal towards all, as may be; reserving the bestowing of their best and greatest love, till they see, where God bestows his. And if so be they cannot, or will not command their inordinate affections, as they should, yet it is widsom to conceal them from their children, whom else they may hurt so many ways; as the ape is said, many times to kill her young ones by too strait embracing them.

The Lord promises and affords long life to such as "honour father and mother,'' Exod. xx. 12; whose days if he shorten in this life for their good, he lengthens out with immortality in glory. On the other side, he cuts off from the earth stubborn and disobedient children suddenly and in sundry ways. And if he give them long life, it is for a curse unto them. They also often die without children themselves; and if not, their children oftener pay them that which is due, and owing them from their parents. The history is note-worthy of the father, who being drawn by his son to the threshold of the house, by the hair of the head; cried to him, to draw him no further, for that he had drawn his father no further. And how should they expect honour from their children who have dishonoured their parents? or a happy life, who despise the author of their life under God? This honour is due not only to them by whom we have our being; but to them also by whom our well-being is furthered.

Growing up in colonial New England was not easy. Rules, laws, and restraints abounded to try to prevent the child born in original sin from falling deeper into mortal sin. The following laws from the 1672 codification of the Massachusetts Bay Colony were copied widely by the other New England colonies in the 17th century, creating a solid wall of order around New English children. It should be noted that the "stubborn child" law of 1646—which is still on the books in Massachusetts—was a capital law, punishable by death. Although no child was ever executed under the law, one young man came very close, as the graphic case of John Porter reveals. The laws are printed in W. H. Whitmore's edition of The Colonial Laws of Massachusetts *(Boston, 1889), pp. 129, 136-137. John's case may be traced in the* Records and Files of the Quarterly Courts of Essex County Massachusetts *(Salem, 1911-21), vol. 2, pp. 336-338, and the* Records of the Governor and Company of the Massachusetts Bay in New England *(Boston, 1853-54), vol. 4:2, pp. 216-217.*

CHILDREN & YOUTH

Forasmuch as the good education of children is of singular behoofe & benefitt to any Common-wealth, & whereas many parents & masters are too indulgent & negligent of their duty in that kind. It is Ordered that the Select men of every Town, in the several precincts, and quarters where they dwel, shal have a vigilant eye over their brethren and neighbours to see, first that none of them shall suffer so much barbarism in any of their families, as not to endeavour to teach, by themselves or others, their children & apprentices, so much learning, as may enable them perfectly to read the english tongue, & knowledg of the Capital laws; upon penaltie of twenty shillings for each neglect therein. Also that all masters of families, do once a week (at the least) catachise their children and servants in the grounds and principles of Religion, & if any be unable to do so much; that then at the least they procure such children and apprentices, to learn some short orthodox catachism without book [i.e. by memory], that they may be able to answer unto the questions, that shall be propounded to them, out of such catachism by their parents or masters or any of the Selectmen, when they shall call them to a tryall, of what they have learned in this kind. And further that all parents & masters do breed & bring up their children & apprentices in some honest Lawfull calling, labour, or imployment, either in husbandry or some other trade, profitable for themselves and the Common-wealth, if they will not, or cannot train them up in learning to fitt them for higher imployments. And if any of the Selectmen after admonition by them given to such masters of families shall find them stil negligent of their duty in the particulars afore mentioned, whereby children & servants become rude, stubborn & unruly, the sayd Select men with the help of two Magistrates or the next County Court for that Shire, shall take such children or apprentices from them, and place them with some masters for yeares, (boyes till they come to twenty one, & girls eighteen years of age compleat) which will more strictly look unto, & force them to submit unto government, according to the Rules of this order, if by fair meanes & former instructions they will not be drawn unto it. [1642]

2. *Forasmuch as it appeareth, by too much experience, that diverse children and servants doe behave themselves disobediently & disorderly, towards their parents, masters, & Governours, to the disturbance of families, &* discouragment of such parents & Governours. It is Ordered by this Court & Authority thereof. That it shall be in the power of any one Magistrate, by warrant directed to the Constable of that Town, where such offender dwels, upon complaint, to call before him any such offender, & upon conviction of such misdemeanors, to sentence him to endure such Corporal punishment, by whipping or otherwise, as in his judgment the merit of the fact shall deserve, not exceeding ten stripes for one offence, or bind the

offender to make his appearance at the next County Court; And further it is also Ordered, That the Commissioners of *Boston* and the three Commissioners of each towne, where no Magistrate dwels, shall have the like power, provided that the person or persons so sentenced, shall have liberty to make their appeale to the next County Court, in any such cases.

3. *Upon information of diverse loose, vaine and corrupt persons, both such as come from forraine parts, as also some, others here inhabiting or residing, which insinuate themselves into the fellowship, of the young people of this Country, drawing them both by night, and by day, from their callings, studyes, and honest occupations,* & lodging places, to the dishonour of God and greif of their *parents, Masters, Teachers, Tutors, Guardians, Overseers* &c: It is Ordered by this Court and the Authority therof. That whosoever shall any wayes cause or suffer any young people or persons whatsoever whether children, servants, apprentices, schollers belonging to the Colledg, or any Latine schoole, to spend any of their time or estate, by night or day, in his or their company, ship or other vessel, shop or house, whether Ordinary, Tavern, victualing house, cellar or other place where they have to do, and shall not from time to time, discharge and hasten all such youths, to their several imployments & places of abode, or lodging aforesayd, if their being in any such place, be known to them, or any other servant or help in the family, or supplying the place of a servant at sea or on land, that then such persons, housholder, shop-keeper, ship-master, ordinary-keeper, taverner, victualler, or other shall forfeith the sum of *forty shillings* upon legal conviction before any Magistrate, or the commissioners authorized to end small causes, one half to the informer, the other half to the Country; and all Constables in their several limits, are required to act herein as is provided in reference to the Law concerning inkeepers.

4. *Whereas sundry Gentlemen of quality, and others, oft times send over their children into this Country, to some freinds here, hoping (at least) thereby to prevent their extravagant and riotous courses, who notwithstanding (by meanes of some unadvised or ill affected persons, which give them credit, in expectation their freinds, either in favour to them, or prevention of blemish to themselves, will discharge their debts) they are no less lavish and profuse here, to the great greife of their freinds, dishonour of God, reproach of the Country*. It is therefore Ordered by this Court. That if any person after

publication hereof, shall any way give credit to any such youth, or other person under one & twenty yeares of age, without order from their freinds here or elswhere, under their hands in writing, they shall loose their debt whatever it be; And further, if such youth or person, incur any penalty by such means and have not wherewith to pay, such person or persons, as are occasions thereof, shall pay it, as delinquents in the like case should doe. [1647]

5. If any person shall wilfully and unreasonably deny any child, timely or convenient marriage, or shall exercise any unnatural severity toward them, such children shall have liberty to complaine to Authority for redress in such cases. [1641]

6. No Orphan, during their minority, which was not committed to tuition or service by their Parents in their life time, shall afterwards be absolutely disposed of by any, without the consent of some Court, wherin two Assistants (at least) shall be present, except in case of marriage, in which the approbation of the major part of the Select men in that Town, or any one of the next Assistants shall be sufficient, and the minority of women in case of marriage, shall be sixteen yeares. [1646]

[CAPITAL LAWS]

13. If any child, or children above sixteen years old, and of sufficient understanding, shall CURSE, or SMITE their natural FATHER, or MOTHER, he or they shall be putt to death, unles it can be sufficiently testifyed, that the Parents have been very unchristianly negligent in the education of such children: or so provoked them by extream & cruel correction, that they have been forced there unto, to preserve themselves from death or maiming: *Exod* 21, 17, *Lev* 20, 9, *Exod* 21, 15.

14. If a man have a STUBBORNE or REBELLIOUS SON of sufficient yeares and understanding (*viz*) sixteen yeares of age, which will not obey the voice of his Father, or the voyce of his Mother, and that when they have chastned him, will not hearken unto them, then shall his Father and Mother, being his natural Parents, lay hold on him, and bring him to the Magistrates assembled in Court, and testifie unto them, that their Son is stubborn and rebellious, and will not obey their voyce and chastisement, but lives in sundry notorious crimes: Such a Son shall be put to death. *Deut*: 22, 20, 21. [1646]

John Porter, jr., having been bound over to this court to answer for his profane, unnatural and abusive carriages to his natural parents, and for abusing authority, the court ordered that he be committed to the house of correction and kept there, according to the rules of the house, until next Ipswich court, and then to be bound to good behavior or continued in the house of correction, as the court shall see cause.

"Novembr the 18: 1661

"Deare & Lo: father

"Sr : These few Laines In the absence of my Poor exiled selfe yor Sonn; though as now things stande yor prisoner, may they in ye roome of my selfe; finde favr in yor eyes, unto which end they bee principally designed are to present you with my humble & childe like duty, tendering the same to my Deare mother, giveing you both to understande; that to my great heart; greife, I Lament that Strange Distance that is beetween you & my poore Slefe; I Say Distance because though, wee are not manny miles a Partt in Respect of Place; yet by Reason of my not beeing Suffered to visitt my fathers house, & my father not chsuseing to come neare his Poor childe; to wch I may add both what I have already and might have; or may suffer, in respectt of present Diffirences I may well tirme it a Strange Distance; and truely among the many Sad Disasters that both by Sea & Land I have to my both Losse & greife mett with all, I Can assuredly affirme, that not one of them all, yea not all put together, have halfe so much aggreived, troubled, or Sadned my Spirits as this present uncomfortable & I may say Dolefull falling out between yor Selfe & me; Whirefore be Pleased to understand that though throug mercy the Prison hath not been my grindeing place; yett With as reall humility and unfeigned submission, I Desier from my Soule to make my peace with you, as If I had Suffired the Shame, & Undergone the Penury which Poor Prisoners in the Common gole mett with, Now Deare Sr lett not yor Spiritt Disdayne to accept of my reall Desier of; being reconciled to you & my mother, nor Let any by respects holde you of from beeing willing to imbrace him; who from his very heartte Laments, his unworthy & untoward Deportment to yor selfe Craveing yor Candor in being, as redy to forgive & forgett, as I am to acknowledge conffesse & forsake yea to Deteste & : abhor all my miscarriages I have onely this to add; that I would not have you thinke, I am yor Late, I will not say, on my Parte; undeserved proceedings; Constreyned to humble my selfe in this manner; but Its the reall Sence of my Dutye & hearty Sorrow for my Slightings of my Parents

wch I hope had not this course at all been taken, both Natur: & grace
would have requiered; But Since it is other wise; I must Proffesse I
begg yor pardon; & doe Entreate you For Loves Sake, For freinds
sake, for gods Sake, to Passe it by, Promiseing in the word of A true
Childe, for futr, Soe to Cary my Selfe wth gods gracecious assitance
as yt I hope I may meritt yor & my mothers Love, at least not incur
yor Displeasure, wch is yt I doe greatly Lament, I should be glad to
see yor Faces & If this may bee acceptable I hope to be soe happy as
in all Love to make an end of all Differences ells with out Extremity
Suits or Law; this with my Duty to you both I rest yor

"Dutyfull Sonn
"John Porter."*

Petition of John Porter, jr.,* to the court: "Whereas your poore
petitioner hath shamefully abused his Father, and mother, contrary
to the very light of nature & much more contrary to the litle light of
the word of God, which he hath bestowed on me (that with shame I
may speake it) haveing had, & enjoyed, such means as I have had, for
so many yeares both in the publick ministry and in my fathers family
also; that your petitioner is in some [small] measure sensible, of that
unparrallell offence that I have justly given to my parents, to others,
of my freinds, to the Commissioners, whome I did shamefully abuse,
I am very sorry that I should so far forget my selfe, and the right
rules, both of God [and] man, though I doe acknowledge I am in
noe measure humbled according to the desert of my great offences,
yet with that small touch God hath been pleased (I hope in mercy) to
give me, of such haynous provokeations I doe upon the bended knees
of my soule, with shame of heart humbley beg pardon of the almighty, who might have consumed me long agon, and I doe humbly
(and I hope through grace) from my heart request the favour of my
parents that they would over looke my unworthy abusive carriage
and behavior toward them, and your poore Petitioner doth humbly
beg forgiveness of this honoured Court of these my greate offences,
and doe hope through the grace of God in Jesus Christ that neither
my parents nor this honoured Court, shall ever have anything of this
nature, to complaine, but that your poore petitioner shall through the
same grace behave himselfe respectfully, to all authority, and with
humble dutye unto my parents, and so to all other relations as I am
concerned in, and shall be forever further oblidged to this honoured
court for this your so great clemency.

Morgan Jones deposed on 30: 8: 1661, that he heard John Porter, the younger, abuse his father and mother within the year. In the month of September, he abused him in these words. saying "thou Robin Hood; thou Hipocrite; thou art a good member thou art a Fit grand juryman," etc. He also said to his mother "your tongue goes like a perriemonger," etc., and on Oct. 4, he called her a hypocrite. His father, delivering him a warrant that morning, said John Porter took it, broke it to pieces, uttering words in contempt of authority, saying that he cared not for Hathorne and his commissioners. Joseph Porter deposed the same and that said John called Hathorne and Batter vile names, saying that they had sent a warrant for him but "I will not goe beffore them: I will goe before Better men then they be." Sworn, 30: 8: 1661, before the commissioners.

Boston, the 30th of May, 1665.

A narrative of the case of John Porter, Juñ.

John Porter, Junior, the sonne of John Porter, of Salem, in the county of Essex, in New England, yeoman, being about thirty yeares of age, & of sufficient capacity to understand his duty unto his superiors, according to the fifth comandment, but he, being instigated by the divill, & his currupt heart destitute of the feare of God, did not only prodigally wast & riotuously expend about fower hundred pounds of money & goods comitted to him by his ffather, for his improovement in two voiages to the Berbadoes, & so for England, where by his evill courses he ran himself further into debt, (& was there imprisoned, from whence being relieved by the charritable assistance of some ffreinds of his ffather,) all which debts his father did voluntarily discharge. After this, returning to New England, his parents enterteined him wth love & tendernes as their eldest sonne, & provided for him as was expedient & necessary. All these things have been clearly demonstrated to the Court; but notwthstanding the sajd John Porter, Juñ, did carry himself very perversly, stubbornely, & rebelliously towards his naturall parents, who are persons of good repute for piety, honesty, & estate.

He called his father theife, lyar, & simple ape, shittabed. Frequently he threatned to burne his fathers house, to cutt doune his house & barne, to kill his catle & horses, & wth an axe cutt doune his fence severall times, & did set fire of a pyle of wood neere the dwelling house, greatly endangering it, being neere thirty roads.

He called his mother Rambeggur, Gamar Shithouse, Gamar Pissehouse, Gamar Two Shooes, & told hir her tongue went like a peare monger, & said she was the rankest sow in the toune;   these abusive names he used frequently.

He reviled Mr Hauthorne, one of the magistrates, calling him base, corrupt fellow, & said he cared not a turd for him.

He reviled, & abused, & beate his fathers servants, to the endangering of the life of one of them.

*He was prooved to be a vile, prophane, & comon swearer & drunkard; he attempted to stab one of his naturall brethren. All which things are prooved by the oathes of sufficient wittnesses upon record.

In this vile & unsufferable course he continued severall yeares, but more especially the two last yeares, sixty two & sixty three. At length, his father, in the sence of his sonnes wickedness & incorrigiblenes, the dayly danger of himself, his estate, & family, by his meanes, sought releife from authority, first more privately, which was ineffectuall, & afterwards more publickly, before the County Court held at Salem, & by that Court was comitted to the house of correction at Ipswich, where he was kept some time; & afterward, being set at liberty, did persist in his former; wicked course, & being againe complained of by his father to the said Salem Court the fower & twentieth of the ninth moneth, 1663, where his offences being found to be of a high nature, he was comitted to prison at Boston, there to remaine for a triall at the Court of Asistants, where he was called to answer upon the fowerth of March, 1663.

The complaints against him, the said Porter, were produced, the wittnesses brought face to face, & his charge prooved; also, his oune naturall father openly complained of the stubbornes & rebellion of this his sonne, & craved justice & releife against him, being over pressed thereunto by his unheard of & unparrelled outrages before named. Unto wch complaints the said John Porter, Juñ, had liberty to answer for himselfe. He impudently denied some things, others he excused by vaine pretences, & some he ouned, but gave no signe of true repentance; wherupon the said Court proceeded to give sentence against him, the sume whereof is, to stand upon the ladder at the gallowes, wth a roape about his neck, for one hower, & afterwards to be severely whipt, & so comitted to the house of correction, to be kept closely to worke, wth the diet of that house, & not thence to be releast wthout speciall order from the Court of Asistants or the Generall

Court, & to pay to the country as a fine two hundred pounds.

If the mother of the said Porter had not been overmooved by hir tender & motherly affections to forbear, but had joyned wth his father in complaining & craving justice, the Court must necessarily have proceeded wth him as a capitall offendor, according to our law, being grounded upon & expressed in the word of God, in Deut̄ 22: 20, 21. See Capital Lawes, p. 9, sect̄ 14.

The children of New England learned to behave properly from many sources—parents, teachers, and ministers—but their earliest written introduction to the accepted rules and standards of their society came from The New England Primer, *the most popular schoolbook in America for over 150 years. The first book for children learning to read, it contained the alphabet, syllables, numbers, word lists, short sayings, moral lessons, and religious creeds. The following lessons are taken from the 1727 Boston edition which Paul Leicester Ford reprinted in 1897.*

Now the Child being entred in his Letters and Spelling, let him learn these and such like Sentences by Heart, whereby he will be both instructed in his Duty, and encouraged in his Learning.

The Dutiful Child's Promises,

I Will fear GOD, and honour the KING.
I will honour my Father & Mother.
I will Obey my Superiours.
I will Submit to my Elders.
I will Love my Friends.
I will hate no Man.
I will forgive my Enemies, and pray to God for them.
I will as much as in me lies keep all God's Holy Commandments.
I will learn my Catechism.
I will keep the Lord's Day Holy.
I will Reverence God's Sanctuary, For our GOD is a consuming Fire.

An Alphabet of Lessons for Youth.

A Wise Son makes a glad Father, but a foolish Son is the heaviness of his Mother.

Better is a little with the fear of the Lord, than great treasure and trouble therewith.

Come unto CHRIST all ye that labour and are heavy laden, and He will give you rest.

Do not the abominable thing which I hate, saith the Lord.

Except a Man be born again, he cannot see the Kingdom of God.

Foolishness is bound up in the heart of a Child, but the rod of Correction shall drive it far from him.

Grieve not the Holy Spirit.

Holiness becomes God's House for ever.

It is good for me to draw near unto God.

Keep thy Heart with all Diligence, for out of it are the issues of Life.

Liars shall have their part in the lake which burns with fire and brimstone.

Many are the Afflictions of the Righteous, but the Lord delivers them out of them all.

Now is the accepted time, now is the day of salvation.

Out of the abundance of the heart the mouth speaketh.

Pray to thy Father which is in secret, and thy Father which sees in secret, shall reward thee openly.

Quit you like Men, be strong, stand last in the Faith.

Remember thy Creator in the days of thy Youth.

Salvation belongeth to the Lord.

Trust in God at all times ye people, pour out your hearts before him.

Upon the wicked God shall rain an horrible Tempest.

Wo to the wicked, it shall be ill with him, for the reward of his hands shall be given him.

eXhort one another daily while is is called to day, lest any of you be hardened through the deceitfulness of Sin.

Young Men ye have overcome the wicked one.

Zeal hath consumed me, because my enemies have forgotten the words of God.   *Choice Sentences.*

1. Praying will make thee leave sinning, or sinning will make thee leave praying.

2. Our Weakness and Inabilities break not the bond of our Duties.

3. What we are afraid to speak before Men, we should be afraid to think before God.

DUTY OF CHILDREN TOWARDS
THEIR PARENTS.

God hath commanded saying, Honour thy Father and Mother, and whoso curseth Father or Mother, let him die the Death. Mat. 15. 4.

Children obey your Parents in the Lord, for this is right.

2. Honour thy Father and Mother, (which is the first Commandment with Promise).

3. That it may be well with thee, and that thou mayst live long on the Earth.

Children, obey your Parents in all Things, for that is well pleasing unto the Lord. Col. 3, 20.

The Eye that mocketh his Father, and despiseth the Instruction of his Mother, let the Ravens of the Valley pluck it out, and the young Eagles eat it.

Father, I have sinned against Heaven, and before thee. Luke 15, 10.

19. I am no more worthy to be called thy Son.

No man ever hated his own flesh, but nourisheth and cherisheth it. Ephes. 5, 19.

I pray thee let my Father and Mother come and abide with you, till I know what God will do for me. I Sam. 22, 3.

My Son, help thy Father in his Age, and grieve him not as long as he liveth.

12. And if his Understanding fail, have patience with him, and despise him not when thou art in thy full Strength.

Whoso curseth his Father or his Mother, his Lamp shall be put out in obscure Darkness. Prov. 20, 20.

Verses.

> I in the Burying Place may see
>   Graves shorter there than I;
> From Death's Arrest no Age is free,
>   Young Children too may die;
> My God, may such an awful Sight,
>   Awakening be to me!
> Oh! that by early Grace I might
>   For Death prepared be.

Puritan New England was the most education-minded society of its day. Only six years after the Massachusetts Bay Colony was first settled in 1630, the Puritan leaders founded Harvard College to provide higher education for the colony's future leaders. And six years after that, in 1642, the Massachusetts legislature passed the first compulsory education law in America. (See the first section of the laws concerning "Children and Youth" on p. 53.) The following three documents illustrate the strenuous Puritan concern for education. The first document is a modernized version of the Massachusetts law of 11 November 1647 which appears in the Records of the Governor and Company of the Massachusetts Bay in New England *(Boston, 1853-54), vol. 2, p. 203. The second is an autobiographical account of New England school life by a future president of Harvard University, Josiah Quincy (1772-1864). Although it was written at the end of the 18th century and about a private academy, it speaks characteristically for the public schools of the whole colonial period in New England. It appears in Edmund Quincy's* Life of Josiah Quincy *(Boston, 1869), pp. 24-25.*

1647: 11 November. It being one chief project of that old deluder, Satan, to keep men from the knowledge of the Scriptures, as in former times by keeping them in an unknown tongue, so in these latter times by persuading from the use of tongues, that so at least the true sense and meaning of the original might be clouded by false glosses of saint seeming deceivers, that learning may not be buried in the grave of our fathers in the church and commonwealth, the Lord assisting our endeavors,—

It is therefore ordered, that every township in this jurisdiction, after the Lord hath increased them to the number of 50 householders, shall then forthwith appoint one within their town to teach all such children as shall resort to him to write and read, whose wages shall be paid either by the parents or masters of such children, or by the inhabitants in general, by way of supply [taxes], as the major part of those that order the prudentials [affairs] of the town shall appoint; provided, those that send their children be not oppressed by paying much more than they can have them taught for in other towns; and it is further ordered, that where any town shall increase to the number of 100 families or householders, they shall set up a grammar [Latin] school, the master thereof being able to instruct youth so far as they may be fitted for the university, provided, that if any town neglect the

performance hereof above one year, that every such town shall pay
5 to the next school till they shall perform this order.

"The discipline of the Academy was severe, and to a child, as I
was, disheartening. The Preceptor was distant and haughty in his
manners. I have no recollection of his ever having shown any consideration for my childhood. Fear was the only impression I received
from his treatment of myself and others. I was put at once into the
first book of Cheever's Accidence, and obliged, with the rest of my
classmates, to get by heart passages of a book which I could not,
from my years, possibly understand. My memory was good, and I
had been early initiated, by being drilled in the Assembly's Catechism, into the practice of repeating readily words the meaning of
which I could not by any possibility conceive. I cannot imagine a
more discouraging course of education than that to which I was sub-
jected.

"The truth was, I was an incorrigible lover of sports of every kind.
My heart was in ball and marbles. I needed and loved perpetual activity of body, and with these dispositions I was compelled to sit with
four other boys on the same hard bench, daily, four hours in the
morning and four in the afternoon, and study lessons which I could
not understand. Severe as was my fate, the elasticity of my mind cast
off all recollection of it as soon as school hours were over, and I do
not recollect, nor believe, that I ever made any complaint to my
mother or any one else.

"The chief variety in my studies was that afforded by reading
lessons in the Bible, and in getting by heart Dr. Watts's Hymns for
Children. My memory, though ready, was not tenacious, and the rule
being that there should be no advance until the first book was con-
quered, I was kept in Cheever's Accidence I know not how long. All
I know is, I must have gone over it twenty times before mastering it. I
had been about four years tormented with studies not suited to my
years before my interest in them commenced; but when I began upon
Nepos, Caesar, and Virgil, my repugnance to my classics ceased, and
the Preceptor gradually relaxed in the severity of his discipline, and,
I have no doubt, congratulated himself on its success as seen in the
improvement he was compelled to acknowledge. During the latter
part of my life in the Academy he was as indulgent as a temperament
naturally intolerant and authoritative would permit.''

*Michael Wigglesworth (1631-1705) would be a good candidate
for the award of Most Typical Puritan of New England's first generation. Born in England and educated at Harvard, he wrote the most
popular book of his time, the poetic* Day of Doom, *ministered both
physically and spiritually to the congregation of Malden, Massachusetts for 49 years, and outlived two wives. The following
autobiographical sketch describing his youth in the earliest settlements of New England was published in the* New England Historical
and Genealogical Register, *vol. 17 (1863), pp. 137-139.*

I was born of Godly Parents, that feared ye Lord greatly, even
from their youth, but in an ungodly Place, where ye generality of ye
people rather derided then imitated their piety, in a place where, to
my knowledge, their children had Learnt wickedness betimes, In a
place that was consumed wth fire in a great part of it, after God had
brought them out of it. These godly parents of mine meeting with opposition & persecution for Religion, because they went from their
own Parish Church to hear ye word & Receiv ye Lords supper &c took up
resolutions to pluck up their stakes & remove themselves to New
England, and accordingly they did so, Leaving dear Relations friends
& acquaintace, their native Land, a new built house, a flourishing
Trade, to expose themselves to ye hazzard of ye seas, and to ye Distressing difficulties of a howling wilderness, that they might enjoy
Liberty of Conscience & Christ in his ordinances. And the Lord
brought them hither & Landed them at Charlstown, after many difficulties and hazzards, and me along with them being then a child not
full seven yeers old. After about 7 weeks stay at Charls Town, my
parents removed again by sea to New-Haven in ye month of October.
In our passage thither we were in great Danger by a storm which drove
us upon a Beach of sand where we lay beating til another Tide fetcht
us off; but God carried us to our port in safety. Winter approaching we
dwelt in a cellar partly under ground covered with earth the first winter, But I remember that one great rain brake in upon us & drencht
me so in my bed being asleep that I fell sick upon it; but ye Lord in
mercy spar'd my life & restored my health. When ye next summer
was come I was sent to school to Mr. Ezekiel Cheever who at that
time taught school in his own house, and under him in a year or two I
profited so much through ye blessing of God, that I began to make
Latin & to get forward apace. But God who is infinitely wise and ab-
soluteiy soverain, and gives no account concerning any of his pro-

ceedings, was pleased about this time to visit my father with Lameness which grew upon him more & more to his dying Day, though he liv'd under it 13 years. He wanting help was fain to take me off from school to follow other employments for ye space of 3 or 4 yeers until I had lost all that I had gained in the Latine Tongue. But when I was now in my fourteenth yeer, my Father, who I suppose was not wel satisfied in keeping me from Learning whereto I had been designed from my infancy, & not judging me fit for husbandry, sent me to school again, though at that time I had little or no disposition to it, but I was willing to submit to his authority therein and accordingly I went to school under no small disadvantage & discouragement seing those that were far inferior to me, by my discontinuance now gotten far before me. But in a little time it appeared to be of God, who was pleased to facilitate my work & bless my studies that I soon recovered what I had lost & gained a great deal more, so that in 2 yeers and 3 quarters I was judged fit for ye Colledge and thither I was sent, far from my parents & acquaintace among strangers. But when father and mother both forsook me then the Lord took care of me. It was an act of great self Denial in my father that notwithstanding his own Lameness and great weakness of Body wch required the service & helpfulness of a son, and having but one son to be ye staff of his age & supporter of his weakness he would yet for my good be content to deny himself of that comfort and Assistance I might have Lent him. It was also an evident proof of a strong Faith in him, in that he durst adventure to send me to ye Colledge, though his Estate was but small & little enough to maintain himself & small family left at home. And God Let him Live to see how acceptable to himself this service was in giving up his only son to ye Lord and bringing him up to Learning; especially ye Lively actings of his faith & self denial herein. For first notwithstanding his great weakness of body, yet he Lived till I was so far brought up as that I was called to be a fellow of ye Colledge and improved in Publick service there, and until I had preached several Times; yea and more then so, he Lived to see & hear what God had done for my soul in turning me from Darkness to light & fro the power of Sathan unto God, wch filled his heart ful of joy and thankfulness beyond what can be expressed. And for his outward estate, that was so far from being sunk by what he spent from yeer to yeer upon my education, that in 6 yeers time it was plainly doubled, wch himself took great notice of, and spake of it to myself and others, to ye praise of

God, wth Admiration and thankfulness. And after he had lived under great & sore affliction for ye space of 13 yeers a pattern of faith, patience, humility & heavenly mindedness, having done his work in my education and receivd an answer to his prayers God took him to his Heavenly Rest where he is now reaping ye fruit of his Labors. When I came first to ye Colledge, I had indeed enjoyed ye benefit of Religious & strict education, and God in his mercy and pitty kept me from scandalous sins before I came thither & after I came there, but alas I had a naughty vile heart and was acted by corrupt nature & therefore could propound no Right and noble ends to myself, but acted from self and for self. I was indeed studious and strove to outdoe my compeers, but it was for honor & applause & prefermt & such poor Beggarly ends. Thus I had my Ends and God had his Ends far differing from mine, yet it pleased him to Bless my studies, & to make me grow in Knowledge both in ye tongues & Inferior Arts & also in Divinity. But when I had been there about three yeers and a half; God in his Love & Pitty to my soul wrought a great change in me, both in heart & Life, and from that time forward I learnt to study with God and for God. And whereas before that, I had thoughts of applying myself to ye study & Practice of Physick, I wholy laid aside those thoughts, and did chuse to serve Christ in ye work of ye ministry if he would please to fit me for it & to accept of my service in that great work.

III. LOVE AND MARRIAGE

The Puritans have long been considered models of prudery and antiromanticism. In what ways were they concerned about sexual morality? What social institutions were responsible for its regulation? How successful were they? What do you think were their standards of "success"? Did they change over time? Why? In what ways were the Puritans romantic and sexually uninhibited? What were the legal conditions for a successful marriage? Were parents involved in their children's choices? At what age did New Englanders marry? Did it change over time? Why? In a day of ineffective contraception, did people make love before marriage? How do we know? Did the recorded patterns of prenuptual intercourse vary over time? What might account for these variations? Was all prenuptual intercourse regarded in the same way? What happened to children born out of wedlock? Who was responsible for their support?

Michael Wigglesworth's first wife died only three years after their marriage in 1655 and he did not remarry for twenty years. His second wife died in 1690, leaving him with seven children. The following document is the result of his courtship of his third wife, Sybil Avery, a physician's widow and the mother of three children. It appears in the New England Historical and Genealogical Register, *vol. 17 (1863), pp. 140-142.*

    Mrs. Avery
& my very kind friend.
    I heartily salute you in ye Lord with many thanks for yor kind entertainment when I was with you March 2d. I have made bold once

more to visit you by a few lines in ye inclosed paper, not to prevent a personal visit, but rather to make way for it, which I fully intend the beginning of ye next week if weather and health Prevent not, craving the favor that you will not be from home at that Time, yet if yor occasions cannot comply with that Time, I shall endeavor to wait upon you at any other Time that may suit you better. Not further to trouble you at this Time, but only to present ye inclosed to yor serious thoughts, I commend both it & you to ye Lord & wait for an Answer from Heaven in due season, meanwhile I am & shall remain,   Yor True Friend

                                            & wel—wisher,

Maldon March 23, 1691.   Michael Wigglesworth.

I make bold to spread before you these following considerations which Possibly may help to clear up yor way before yu return an answer unto ye Motion wch I have made to you, I hope you will take them in good Part, and Ponder them seriously.

1st. I have a great perswasion that ye motion is of God, for diverse Reasons.

As first that I should get a little acquaintance with you by a short & transient visit having been altogether a stranger to you before, and that so little acquaintance should leave such impressions behind it, as neither length of Time, distance of Place, nor any other objects could wear off, but that my thoughts & heart have been toward you ever since.

2ly. That upon serious, earnest and frequent seeking of God for guidance & Direction in so weighty a matter, my thoughts have still been determined unto and fixed upon yorself as the most suitable Person for me.

3ly. In that I have not been led hereunto by fancy (as too many are in like cases) but by sound Reason & judgment, Principally Loving and desiring you for those gifts & graces God hath bestowed upon you, and Propounding ye Glory of God, the adorning and furtherance of ye Gospel. The spiritual as wel as outward good of myself and family, together wth ye good of yorself & children, as my Ends inducing me hereunto.

2ly. Be Pleased to Consider, that although you may Peradventure have offers made you by Persons more Eligible, yet you can hardly meet with one that can love you better, or whose love is built upon a surer foundation, or that may be capable of doing more for you in some respects than myself. But let this be spoken with all humility, & without ostentation. I can never think meanly enough of myself.

3ly. Whither there be not a great sutableness in it for one that hath been a Physician's wife to match with a Physician [Wigglesworth was a sickly man and consequently devoted much of his time in Maldon to the study and practice of medicine]. By this means you may in some things & at some Times afford more help than another, & in like manner receive help, get an increase of skill, and become capable of doing more that way hereafter if need should be.

4ly. Whither God doth not now invite you to ye doing of some more Eminent Service for him, than you are capable of doing in yor Present Private capacity? and whither those many Emptyings from vessel to vessel & great afflictions that have befaln you might not be sent with a design to fit you for further service, & to losen you from ye Place & way you have been in?

5ly. Whither ye enjoyment of Christ in all his ordinances (which at present cannot be had where you are) be not a thing of that weight that may render this motion at this time somewhat more considerable?

6ly. Consider, if you should continue where you are whither ye looking after & managing of yor outward Business &affairs may not be too hard for you, and hazzard your health again?

7ly. If God should exercise you with sickness again whither it were not more comfortable and save to have a neer and dear friend to take care of you and yours at such a Time, especially now when yor dear mother is gone to Heaven.

8ly. This following summer is Likely to be full of Troubles (unless God prevent beyond the expectation of man) by reason of our Indian and French Enemyes: now whither it may not be more comfortable and safe to get neerer ye heart of the Country, than to continue where you are & to live as you do?

9ly. The consideration of ye many afflictions, losses & Bereavements which have befallen you, as it hath affected my heart with deep sympathy, so it hath been no small inducement to me to make this motion, hopeing that if God should give it acceptance with you I might be a friend & a Comforter to you instead of yor many lost relations; and I hope upon trial you would find it so.

10ly. As my Late wife was a means under God of my recovering a better state of Health; so who knows but God may make you instrumental to Preserve & Prolong my health & life to do him service.

Obj. As to that main objection in respect to my Age, I can say nothing to that, But my Times are in the hands of God, who as he hath restored my health beyond expectation, can also if he Please Prolong it while he hath any service for me to do for his Name. And in ye mean time, if God shall Please and yourself be willing to Put me in that Capacity, I hope I shall do you as much Good in a little time as it is Possible for me to do, & use some endeavours also to Provide for yor future, as wel as Present, welfare, as God's Bounty shall enable me; for true love cannot be idle.

Ob. And for ye other objection from ye number of my children & difficulty of guiding such a family. 1st. the Number may be lessened if there be need of it.

2ly. I shall gladly improve my authority to strengthen yours (if God shall so Perswade your heart) to do what lieth in me to make the burden as light & comfortable as may be. And I am perswaded there would be a great suitableness in our tempers, spirits, Principles, & consequently a sweet and harmonious agreement in those matters (& in all other matters) betwixt us, and indeed this Perswasion is a Principle thing wch hath induced me to make this motion to yorself & to no other.

Finally that I be not over tedious, I have great hope, that if God shall Perswade you to close with this motion, the Consequents will be for ye furthurance of ye Gospel, for ye Comfort of us both, & of both our familyes & that ye Lord will make us mutual helpers & Blessings to each other, & that we shall enjoy much of God together in such a Relation, without which no relation can be truly sweet.

If the courtship of a New England couple was successful, the next step was often an elaborate marriage contract, such as that between Jacob Mygatt and Sarah Whiting of Hartford, Connecticut in 1654. Their original contract is printed in the Collections of the Connecticut Historical Society, *vol. 14 (1912), pp. 558-560.*

Whereas I, Joseph Mygatt, of Hartford upon the River and in the jurisdiction of Connecticut in New England, have in the behalf of my son Jacob and at his request made a motion to Mrs. Susanna Fitch, in reference to her daughter Sarah Whiting, that my said son Jacob might with her good liking have free liberty to endeavor the gaining of her said daughter Sarah's affection towards himself in a way of marriage: now this present writing showeth that the said Mrs. Susanna Fitch having consented thereunto, I do hereby promise and engage that if God, in the wise disposition of His providence, shall so order it that my son Jacob and her daughter Sarah shall be contracted together in reference to marriage, I will pay thereupon unto my said son as his marriage portion the full sum of two hundred pounds sterling, upon a just valuation in such pay as shall be to the reasonable satisfaction of the said Mrs. Fitch, and so much more as shall fully equalize the estate or portion belonging to her said daughter Sarah. And I do further engage for the present to build a comfortable dwelling house for my said son and her daughter to live in by themselves, as shall upon a true account cost me fifty pounds sterling. And [I] will also give them therewith near the said house one acre of ground planted with apple trees and other fruit trees, which said house, land, and trees shall be and remain to my said son as an addition to his marriage portion, before mentioned, and to his heirs forever. And I do also further promise and engage that at the day of my death I shall and will leave unto him my said son and his heirs so much estate besides the dwelling house, ground, and trees, before given and engaged, as shall make the two hundred pounds, before engaged and to be paid [at] present, more than double the portion of the said Sarah Whiting. And for the true and sure performance hereof I do hereby engage and bind over my dwelling house and all my lands and buildings in Hartford, with whatsoever estate in any kind is therein and thereupon. And I do further engage that my daughter Mary's portion of one hundred pounds being first paid to her, I will leave to my said son and his heirs forever my whole estate at the day of my death, whatsoever it shall amount unto, and in what way, kind, or place soever it lies, he paying to my wife during her natural life twelve pounds a year, and allowing to her a dwelling entire to herself in the two upper rooms and cellar belonging to my now dwelling house, with the going of half the poultry and a pig for her comfort in each year during her said life, also allowing her the use of half the household stuff during her life, which she shall have power to dispose of to Jacob or Mary at her death, as she shall see cause. And I do further engage that the portion my said son shall have with her daughter Sarah shall (with the good liking of the said Mrs. Susanna Fitch and such friends as she shall advise with) be laid out wholly upon a farm for the sole use and benefit of my said son, her daughter, and their heirs forever. And upon the contraction in reference to marriage I do engage to jointure her said daughter Sarah in the whole estate or portion my son hath with her, laid out or to be laid out in a farm as aforesaid or otherwise, and in the thirds of his whole estate otherwise, to be to her sole and proper use and benefit during her life and after her death to their heirs forever. And lastly I do engage that the whole benefit of the Indian trade shall be to the sole advantage of my son Jacob, and do promise that I will during my life be [an] assistant and helpful to my said son in the best ways I can, both in his trading with the Indians, his stilling, and otherwise, for his comfort and advantage which I will never bring to any account with him; only I do explain myself and engage that in case my son Jacob shall depart this life before her daughter Sarah, and leave no issue of their bodies, then her said daughter Sarah shall have the full value of her portion left to her, not only for her life as before, but to her as her property to dispose of at her death as she shall see cause, and her thirds in all his other estate for her life, as is before expressed. It being also agreed and consented to that my wife after my decease and during her natural life shall have the use of two milch cows which my son Jacob shall provide for her, she paying the charge of their wintering and summering out of her annuity of twelve pounds a year. In witness whereunto, and to every particular on this and the other side, I have subscribed my name, this 27th of November, 1654.

Witnesses hereunto

John Webster
John Cullick
John Tallcott
The mark of
    J M
Joseph Mygatt

The age at which colonial New Englanders married varied from town to town and decade to decade, but the following statistics give some indication of the directions in which marriage ages were moving. Tables 3 and 4 come from Philip Greven's study of Four Generations *in colonial Andover, Massachusetts (Ithaca, 1970), pp. 207, 209; Table 5 is the product of John Demos's study of family life in Plymouth Colony entitled* A Little Commonwealth *(New York, 1970), p. 193.*

Table 3. Age at marriage of second-, third-, and fourth-generation males
in Andover, Massachusetts.

Age	Second generation No.	%	Third generation No.	%	Fourth generation No.	%
Under 21	5	4.8	6	2.7	17	5.8
21-24	36	34.6	72	32.1	122	41.5
25-29	39	37.5	87	38.8	119	40.5
30-34	17	16.3	39	17.4	27	9.2
35-39	4	3.8	12	5.4	6	2.0
40 and over	3	2.9	8	3.6	3	1.0
Total	104	99.9	224	100.0	294	100.0

Table 4. Age at marriage of second-, third-, and fourth generation females
in Andover, Massachusetts.

Age	Second generation No.	%	Third generation No.	%	Fourth generation No.	%
Under 21	29	35.8	58	27.6	90	31.9
21-24	32	39.5	74	35.2	105	37.2
25-29	14	17.3	48	22.9	60	21.3
30-34	3	3.7	12	5.7	18	6.4
35-39	2	2.5	10	4.8	5	1.8
40 and over	1	1.2	8	3.8	4	1.4
Total	81	100.0	210	100.0	282	100.0

Table 5:

FIRST MARRIAGES IN PLYMOUTH COLONY

	Born Before 1600	Born 1600-25	Born 1625-50	Born 1650-75	Born 1675-1700
Mean age of men at time of first marriage	27.0	27.0	26.1	25.4	24.6
Mean age of women at time of first marriage	—	20.6	20.2	21.3	22.3
Percentage of men married at age 23 or under	25	18	25	26	38
Percentage of men married at age 30 or over	44	23	27	18	14
Percentage of women married at age 25 or over	—	9	10	20	28

Note: The sample on which this table is based comprises a total of 650 persons. There is, however, insufficient data for women born before 1600.

Courting customs have always had an amusing side, and the peculiar New England custom of "tarrying" (often called "bundling" by the locals) was no exception. It was described by the Rev. Andrew Burnaby, a visiting Anglican minister, in his Travels through the Middle Settlements in North-America in the Years 1759 and 1760 *(2nd ed. London, 1775; reprinted Ithaca, 1960), pp. 102-103.*

Singular situations and manners will be productive of singular customs; but frequently such as upon slight examination may appear to be the effects of mere grossness of character, will, upon deeper research, be found to proceed from simplicity and innocence. A very extraordinary method of courtship, which is sometimes practised amongst the lower people of this province, and is called Tarrying, has given occasion to this reflection. When a man is enamoured of a young woman, and wishes to marry her, he proposes the affair to her parents, (without whose consent no marriage in this colony can take place); if they have no objection, they allow him to tarry with her one night, in order to make his court to her. At their usual time the old couple retire to bed, leaving the young ones to settle matters as they can; who, after having sate up as long as they think proper, get into bed together also, but without pulling off their under-garments, in order to prevent scandal. If the parties agree, it is all very well; the banns are published, and they are married without delay. If not, they part, and possibly never see each other again; unless, which is an accident that seldom happens, the forsaken fair-one prove pregnant, and then the man is obliged to marry her, under pain of excommunication.

Even if the unlucky couple did marry before the birth of their "tarry-child", they were still liable to the threat of excommunication and the civil law besides, as the following order from the Plymouth Colony Court makes clear. It can be found in the Records of the Colony of New Plymouth in New England. *(Boston, 1855-61), vol. 11, p. 95.*

1645: It is enacted by the court and the authoritie thereof that any person or persons that shall committ Carnall copulation before or without lawfull contract shalbee punished by whiping or els pay ten pounds fine a peece and bee Imprisoned during the pleasure of the Court soe it bee not above three daies but if they bee or wilbee married the one to the other then but ten pounds both and Imprisoned as aforsaid; and by a lawfull Contract the Court understands the mutuall concent of parents or guardians if there bee any to bee had and a sollemne promisc of marriage in due time to each other before two competent witnesses; and if any person or persons shall committ Carnall Copulation after contract and before marriage they shall pay each fifty shillings and bee both Imprisoned during the pleasure of the Court soe it bee not above three daies: or els in case they cannot or will not pay the fine then to suffer corporall punishment by whiping;

That the laws and sanctions of New England were no dead letters is demonstrated by the records of the county and church courts which meted out punishments for sexual misdemeanors. The first case is taken from the Records and Files of the Quarterly Courts of Essex County, Massachusetts *(Salem, 1911-21), vol. 4, pp. 38-40. The second group of actions occurred before the Suffolk County Court, whose records for 1671-1680 have been published in the* Publications of the Colonial Society of Massachusetts, *vols. 29-30 (1933). The final records are those of the First Church in Boston for 1630-1868; they too have been published in the* Publications *of the Colonial Society of Massachusetts, vols. 39-41 (1961), pp. 181-183.*

William Reeves and Susana Durin, appearing to answer for committing fornication, which they confessed, said Reeves, having some other misdemeanors charged against him, was sentenced to be severely whipped and to pay 50s. fine and 50s. to Mr. Cromwell for abusing his maid. Susana was sentenced to be severely whipped or pay a fine of 4li. Reeves was bound in 20li. to free the town from the support of the child and in 10li. for good behavior. John Reeves, surety.

Petition of Willm. Reeves: "With all submissive respect prostrating himself at ye feete of yor clemency, Sheweth that whereas he is a prisoner now before you, deservedly detected with an arrest for a crime repugnant to ye law of god & man; wherein he humbly desires to acknowledge ye Justice of god who is ye revealer of secrets & hath made his sin obvious to his shame, wch he humbly beggs of god may so ashame him as to make him have a detestation agt such & all other sins: whereby gods name is dishonord—now I am before you as a poore offendr to be tried according to ye desert of my act, & err long must appeare before him who is ye Judge both of quicke & dead; then woe for me were there not pardon in ye Blood of Jesus; for as to ye law I must owne my self to be inexcusable; ye equity whereof constraining me to silence; onely this yor poore petitioner craves ye favor of liberty to plead for as being left fatherless in this respect to have ye benefitt of him or any such paternall friend to Intercede for ye mittigation of his dreaded sentence; oh that this my fall might turne many from sin; now what yor poore petitioner in his owne behalf hath to say wch he humbly beggs you to take into yor gentle consideration & in charity to beleive as knoweing Between God & his owne conscience to be true; Its not unknowne that I & ye young woman lived servants in a house together unto whom my affections were & still are so deare as to make her my wife & would have Asked for her . . . but being in ye condition that we were both durst not attempt it though I well could perceive my mistress' apprehension concerning such a Thing . . . but my hope is in god who can restrain ye wrath of man; & Blessed be god that you our rulers are not children but men of piety & growth in Christ who is ye president of mercy . . . yor poore petitioner then humbly beseeches you Duely to weigh his case; in that ye young woman now suffering with him may not be with held from him in ye way of marriage & debarred as she is from so much as comeing to see her poore babe, ever since it was stript & Turned naked away from her, wch according to ye bond of meere humanity & nature would be thought Impossible, were there not extraordinary restraint & feare; once more I beseech you wth what Tendernes possible to consider us both & rather to take ye Fine of me, according to law, for this our offence, as being in yor brest, then to have ye Infliction of corporall punishmt''

Thomas Ives, aged about twenty years, deposed that William Reeves said he wondered what ''aileth our maide, for as soone as I come in at the dore she either runeth into ye other roome or up into ye Chamber.'' Reeves also told him that he had a ''Certaine pouder called Love powder a portion whereof he would give to Susanna Durell in some maner of drinke, to cause her to follow him.''

Deponent had heard Susanna say that she wished her mistress would send her out of the house to some other place until Reeves had gone from his master's house. Sworn in court.

Letter, dated July 1, 1668, Martha Slater to Goody Gatchell: "I would Intreate you to speake In my boyes behalfe and to Doe for him as much as if I ware theare present for as much as I am Anciant and not well able to goe my selfe and you knowe that hee is friendlesse you will very much obliege your Friend."

John Rowdin, aged about fifty years, deposed that Will. Reeves told him some scandal concerning the wife of Walter Skiner. Also that Reeves being sent for cattle, came into the house of Robert Coburne with the daughter of Thomas Whiteredge and went out again with her, he being in drink. Sworn, 22: 4: 1668, before Wm. Hathorne, assistant.

Mary Rowden, aged about forty-eight years, deposed that the wife of Walter Skiner kept bad company at Marblehead, etc. Sworn, 22: 4: 1668, before Wm. Hathorne, assistant.

Margery and Sarah Williams deposed that Susana Durin, Mrs. Cromwell's servant, often came to their house and asked Sarah to go over to sit with her when there was nobody at home but Will. Reeves, saying that she could not abide to be with him alone. Sarah Williams had laid with her for more than a year, etc. Sworn, 19: 4: 1668, before Wm. Hathorne, assistant.

Elizabeth Price, aged about fifty-two years, deposed concerning reprimanding Reeves for his conduct.

Robert Colburne, aged about sixty years, and Alice Colburne, aged about sixty years, deposed that Wm. Reeves came to their house about ten o'clock one night with Florence Hart, jr. They desired Reeves to stay and go to bed, but he would not. Afterward he abused strangers upon the road and then they brought him to Colburne's house to bed. Sworn, June 25, 1668, before Daniel Denison.

1672: 30 January. Sarah Carpenter, presented upon strong suspicion of being wth Childe, the Court ordered she should bee Searched by mrs Parker, mrs Williams, & mrs Sands who made return with Goodwife Tailor a midwife, that she was not wth Childe.

Mary Reade, made in Oath in Court this 9th 12mo 1671. [9 February 1672] that the Childe that was born of her Body of wch she was delivered at Hampton was begot by Edwd Naylor & no other man.

30 April. Wm Hawkins presented by the Grand Jurie, for being

principally Instrumentall & privately conveying away in the night [to Barbadoes] Hannah Hoppine without her friends consent who is reported to bee wth Childe.

The Court taking into consideracion the Bastard Childe born at Roxberry begotten by the saide Silvanus [Warro, a Negro slave], They Order that [he] make provicion in paying two shillings six pence per week for its maintenance to save the Towne of Roxberry harmeless from the chardge of that Childe.

Mary Plumm, being committed to Prison for being in the Chamber of Timmo[thy] Connell late at night . . . Acknowledged in Court she was there naked to her Shift where were two men in Bed. Timmo-[thy] Connell convicted for giving Entertainment in his house to men & women in the night in a Suspitious mann[e]r.

1673: 28 January. Martha Stanton being bound over to this Court for her committing Fornicacion & having an illegitimate Childe, which she confessed in Court. Thomas Trott being accused by Martha Stanton to bee the father of her illegitimate Childe; which the saide Thomas Strongly denied & tendred his oath thereof, so that hee not being legally convict[ed] soe to bee, & hee presenting an Attest of severall of his neighbourhood of his good conversation [behaviour] The Court Sentanceth the saide Trot to bee admonished & to pay Fees of Court.

28 October. Dinah Silvester bound over to this Court to Answer for her committing of Fornicacion & haveing a bastard Childe not being in a marriage state; which Shee Owned in Court, chargeing Jonathan Badcock to bee the Father thereof & said hee had fellowship with her but once & that was in October, 1672.

1674: 27 January. [Margaret Preist confessed in court, her bastard child in her arms, that she had committed fornication with Josias Rose.] And the Midwife & other women present with her at her travell [labor and delivery] testifying that Shee did persist in soe chargeing of him, being put to it in her Extremity.

28 April. Elizabeth Wheeler & Joanna Peirce being Summoned to appear before the Court to answer for theire disorderly carriage in the house of Thomas Watts being married women & founde sitting in other mens Laps with theire Armes about theire Necks.

28 July. Edward Peggy being bound over to this Court to answer what should bee alleaged & proved against him for useing indirect meanes by powders or other wayes unlawfull to Engage the affections or desires of women kinde to him & for begetting Ruth Hen-

ningway of Roxbury with Childe . . . for his making Suite to & drawing away the affections of Ruth Henningway; as also the daughter of Robert Sanford without first obteining theire parents consent.

1676: Thomas Jay being presented . . . for Lascivious carriages towards some young persons of the Female kinde. [He was to pay 20 shillings fine] or that then hee stand upon a block or stoole in the market place in Boston with a paper upon his breast written in a Large character *For Lascivious Carriages towards young women.*

1677: 31 July. [Mary Drury, aged 54, gave as her reason for not living with her husband] that she being marryed to Hew Drury, after [the] time of hir marrig I the said mary Dury lo[d]ged with [him] six weekes or thear abouts, in w[h]ich time the said Hew Drury [nev]er had fellow ship with me as a husband thou[gh] he did indevor [it] the two first nites I lay with him he indevored it but he never had fellow ship with me, nor was abull . . .

1678: 30 April. Martha Horcely convict[ed] by her own confession in Court of committing Fornication with William Dogget & Peter Roberts immediately one after another, and in the sight of each other. [She received 20 lashes in Boston and Dorchester each.]

Excommunications etc.

1712: 9 April. Rachel Preson (formerly Draper) having been guilty of Fornication the matter was laid before the Church, and att the same time there was read a Confession of her sin, and a desire of pardon; she was suspended from the Ordinances [sacraments], as a space allowed to give full proof of the sincerity of her repentence, which the Church consented to by a silent vote.

At a Church Meeting at the Meeting House, September 10, 1721. William Booker a Member of this church, having been guilty of fornication, made humble and open confession of his sin before the Church; and they forgave him, and continued him in their communion. At the same time, Rachel Preson (once Draper) formerly admonished and suspended from special ordinances for being guilty of fornication; was upon a penitent Confession of her Sin, forgiven by the Church and restored to communion.

1733: 13 November. A Confession of Elisabeth Dunn a Sister of this Church humbling her self for her Sin, in Breach of the 7th Commandment, by cohabiting with him, who is now her Husband, before Marriage (by whom she had a Child within about 6 Months after it), was read and accepted etc.

The records of individual sexual offences, especially when culled from the whole corpus of legal and ecclesiastical actions, present only a partial picture of the amorous behavior of our ancestors. To obtain a fuller understanding of that behavior it is necessary to turn to the statistical discoveries of historical demographers, who deal with as complete a population as the records allow. John Demos has made a study of the "Families in Colonial Bristol, Rhode Island" (*William and Mary Quarterly*, vol. 25 [1968], pp. 40-57) from which he derived the following table on the incidence of prenuptial pregnancies in one seaport town.

Table 6. Intervals between Marriage and Birth of First Child in Bristol, Rhode Island.

Time of Marriage	Total No. of Couples	Number with First Child Within 8 Months	Percentage with First Child Within 8 Months
1680-1700	19	0	0%
1700-1720	8	0	0%
1720-1740	42	4	10%
1740-1760	35	17	49%
1760-1780	23	10	44%

The demographer draws his statistics from several kinds of records but the most common are town vital records which record all the births, marriages, and deaths that have occurred in that town over the years. The following excerpts from the Vital Records of Rhode Island 1636-1850: *Vol. 6 Bristol County (Providence, 1894) contain all the marriages and births in the Diman family. The way to calculate the incidence of prenuptial pregnancies is to choose the marriage of any couple, count forward 8 months, then find the first child of that marriage, and note its birth date. If the date of birth of the first child falls within the 8-month period after the marriage of the parents, the child was obviously conceived before the wedding ceremony.*

MARRIAGES:

Jeremiah, and Sarah Giddens, (Int.) April 14, 1733; m. by Rev. Barnabus Taylor, May 13, 1733.

Lucretia, and Richard Smith, (Int.) Nov. 28, 1741; m. Dec. 24, 1741.

Nathaniel, and Mrs. Anna Gallup; m. by Rev. John Burt, Oct. 18, 1756.

James, and Mrs. Ann LeFavour; m. by Rev. John Burt, March 30, 1758.

Mrs. Hannah, and George Oxx, Oct. 29, 1761.

Joseph, of Deacon Jeremiah, and Mrs. Margaret DeWolf, daughter of Capt. Mark A.; m. by Rev. John Burt, Nov. 26, 1767.

Jonathan, of Deacon Jeremiah, and Dorothy Fales of Nathaniel; m. by Rev. John Burt, Oct. 17, 1771.

William, of Nathaniel and Anna, and Anna Munro, of Charles and Anna; m. by Rev. Henry Wight, Nov. 11, 1791.

Elizabeth Fales, and Hezekiah Jackson, May 20, 1798.

Jeremiah, of Jonathan and Dorothy, and Rhoda Sandford, of Royal and Rhoda; m. by Rev. Henry Wight, Oct. 4, 1810.

Hannah, and Billings Waldron, Feb. 16, 1812.

Fanny Martin, and Peleg Gardiner Jones, June 26, 1821.

Francis L. D., and Rosabella Barrows; m. by Rev. G. F. Sanborn, May 16, 1842.

Marian, and James P. Pierce, June 13, 1843.

Elizabeth Wl, and Jeremiah W. Munro, Aug. 6, 1846.

Clara Anna, and Algernon Sidney DeWolf, June 30, 1847.

Joanna, and Benjamin H. Whitford, Nov. 29, 1848.

Mrs. Martha, and John Henry Schomacker, May 26, 1851.

James, and Adeline R. Cottrell, of Athens, Vt.; m. by Rev. Asa Kent, Dec. 20, 1855.

BIRTHS:

Nathaniel, of Jeremiah and Sarah,   Jan. 29, 1734.
James,   Oct. 19, 1735.
Sarah,   Feb. 11, 1738.
Jeremiah,   July 13, 1740.
Jonathan,   Oct. 19, 1742.
Hannah,   Oct. 19, 1742.

William,   Dec. 10, 1744.

William, of Nathaniel and Anna (also 4-S1),   Nov. 1, 1759.

Jeremiah,   Jan. 4, 1767.

Royal, of Joseph and Margaret,   May, 26, 1768.

Jeremiah,   March 26, 1770.

Margaret,   Dec. 27, 1773.

Joseph,   Aug. 16, 1785.

Sarah, of Jonathan and Dorothy,   May 2, 1772.

Betsey Fales,   Feb. 20, 1774.

Jonathan,   Sept. 16, 1775.

Willard, of Timothy and Ruth,   Nov. 23, 1781.

John, of Timothy and Elizabeth,   June 24, 1791.

John, of William and Nancy,   Jan. 2, 1794.

James, of Jeremiah, 2d, and Abigail,   March 15, 1795.

Byron, of Jeremiah and Hannah,   Aug. 5, 1795.

George Howe,   Aug. —, 1797.

Francis Moore, of Royal and Elizabeth,   June 8, 1796.

Royal,   April 4, 1798.

Jonathan, of Billings and Hannah (Butts),   Dec. 8, 1812.

Elizabeth Jackson,   Oct. 17, 1814.

George Byron, of Byron and Abby Alden (Wight),   May 16, 1824.

Clara Anna,   April 1, 1828.

Jeremiah Lewis,   May 1, 1831.

Henry Wight,   April 2, 1835.

Abby Byron,   May 7, 1838.

IV. WORK AND PLAY

A lazy Puritan was a bad Puritan. Why was work so important to the Puritans? Why was the choice of an occupation (or calling) important? What role did parents play in this choice? What constituted an inappropriate choice? How did most young people learn their callings? What was the nature of the relationship between master and apprentice? Why was the apprenticeship system subject to abuses? Who was ultimately responsible for the apprentice's welfare? What were some of the common worries of parents who were putting their children out to 'prentice? Were they legitimate? When and how did the Puritans relax from their callings? What recreation did they consider legitimate? What illegitimate? By what standard was the division made? What was the occasion for the first thanksgiving? Was it a religious celebration? Who attended? What was eaten? How long did it last?

Puritans looked to their ministers for intellectual and spiritual guidance, and the most admired Puritan minister was William Perkins (1558-1602), a fellow of Christ's College, Cambridge. His "Treatise of the Vocations or Callings of men" portrayed the Puritan attitude toward work for generations of English and American Puritans. The following excerpts are taken from The Workers of that Famous and Worthy Minister of Christ in the Universitie of Cambridge, Mr. William Perkins *(London, 1626-31), vol. 1, pp. 750-758.*

A vocation or calling, is a certain kind of life, ordained and imposed on man by God, for the common good. . . . There are two generall rules to be learned of all, which belong to every calling. The first: whatsoever any man enterprizeth or doth, either in word or

deede, he must doe it by vertue of his calling, and he must keepe himselfe within the compasse, limits, or precincts thereof. This rule is
laid downe in these wordes of the Apostles: *Let every man abide in
that calling, wherein he was called. . . .* The second generall rule
which must bee remembred, is this: That *Every man must doe the
duties of his calling with diligence. . . .*

And to like purpose our people have a common saying, that an occupation is as good as land, because land may be lost; but skill and
labour in a good occupation is profitable to the end, because it will
helpe at neede, when land and all things faile. And on the other side,
wee must take heede of two damnable sinnes that are contrary to this
diligence. The first is idlenesse, whereby: the duties of our callings,
and the occasions of glorifying God, are neglected or omitted. The
second is slouthfulnes, whereby they are performed slackly and
carelesly. God in the Parable of the hus-bandman, cals them that are
idle into his vineyard, saying, *Why stand ye idle all the day? Mat.
20.6.* And the servant that had received but one talent, is called an
evill servant, because he was slouthfull in the use of it: for so it is
said. *Thou evill servant and alouthful, Mat. 25.26. S. Paul* gives this
rule to the Thessalonians, *He that would not labour, must not eate:*
yet such a one hee would have to bee noted by a letter, as walked
inordinately. And this he sheweth, that slouth and negligence in the
duties of our callings, are a disorder against that comly order which
God hath set in the societies of mankind, both in church and common-wealth. And indeed, idlenes and slouth are the causes of many
damnable sinnes. The idle bodie, and the idle braine, is the shop of
the divell. The sea, if it mooved not, could not but putrifie, and the
body, if it be not stirred and mooved, breedeth diseases. Now the idle
and slouthful person is a sea of corruption; and when he is most idle,
Satan is least idle; for then is he most busie to draw him to manifold
sinnes.

Thus much of the two general rules. Now follow the parts and
kindes of Vocations: and they are of two sorts: Generall, or Particular. The generall calling is the calling of Christianity, which is
common to all that live in the Church of God. The particular, is that
special calling that belongs to some particular men: as the calling of a
Magistrate, the calling of a Minister, the calling of a Master, of a
father, of a childe, of a servant, of a subject, or any other calling that
is common to all. And *Paul* acknowledging this distinction of

Callings, when he saith, *Let every man abide in that calling, wherin he is called*, that is, in that particular and personall calling, in which he was called to bee a Christian. . . .

A personall calling is the execution of some particular office; arising of that distinction which God makes betweene man and man in every societie. First I say, it is *the execution of some particular office;* as for example, the calling of a magistrate is to execute the office of government over his subjects, the office of a minister is to execute the duty of teaching his people, the calling of a master, is to execute the office of authority and government over his servants: the office of a Physition, is to put in practise the good means whereby life and health are preserved. In a word, in every estate the practise and execution of that particular office, wherein any man is placed, is his personall calling.

Secondly I adde, that it ariseth from that distinction which God maketh betweene man and man in every society: to shew what is the foundation and ground of all personall callings. And it is a point to bee considered of us, which I thus explaine: God in his word hath ordained the societie of man with man, partly in the Common-wealth, partly in the Church, and partly in the family: and it is not the will of God that man should live and converse alone by himselfe. Now for the maintaining of society, he hath ordained a certaine bond to linke men together, which Saint *Paul* calleth *the bond of peace, and the bond of perfection*, namely, love. And howsoever hee hath ordained societies, and the bond of them all, yet hath he appointed that there should stil remaine a distinction betweene man and man, not onely in regard of person, but also in other respects: for as the whole bodie is not the hand, nor the foote, nor the eye, but the hand one part, the foot another, and the eye another: and howsoever in the bodie one part is linked to another, yet there is a distinction betwixt the members, whereby it commeth to passe, that the hand is the hand, not the foot, and the foote, the foote, not the hand, nor the eye: so it is in societies; there is a distinction in the members thereof, and that in two respects: first, in regard of the inward gifts which God bestowed on every man, giving to severall men severall gifts according to his good pleasure. Of this distinction in regard of inward gifts, *Paul* intreates at large, *1. Cor. 12.* through the whole chapter, where he sheweth the diversity of gifts that God bestowes on his Church, and so proportionally in every society. Now looke as the inward gifts of men are severed, so are the persons distinguished in their societies accordingly. Secondly, persons are distinguished by order, whereby God hath appointed, that in every society one person should bee above or under another; not making all equall, as though the bodie should bee all head and nothing else: but even in degree and order, hee hath set a distinction, that one should be above another. And by reason of this distinction of men, partly in respect of gifts, partly, in respect of order, come personall callings. For if all men had the same gifts, and all were in the same degree and order, then should all have one and the same calling: but in asmuch as God giveth diversitie of gifts inwardly, and distinction of order outwardly, hence proceede diversitie of personall callings, and therefore I added, that personall callings arise from that distinction which God maketh betweene man and man in every societie. And thus wee see what is a personall calling. Now before I come to intreate of the parts thereof, there bee other generall rules to bee learned, which concerne all personall callings whatsoever.

1. Rule. Every person of every degree, state, sexe, or condition without exception, must have some personall and particular calling to walke in. This appeareth plainly by the whole word of God. *Adam* so soone as he was created, even in his integrity had a personall calling assigned him by God: which was, to dresse and keepe the garden. And after *Adams* fall, the Lord giveth a particular commandement to him and all his posterity, which bindeth all men to walke in some calling, either in the Church or Commonwealth, saying, *Gen. 3.19. In the sweate of thy browes shalt thou eate thy bread.* Againe, in the renewing of the law in mount Sinai, the fourth commaundement doth not onely permit labour on six daies, but also injoynes the same (as I take it) to us all. For Gods example is there propounded for·us to follow, that as he rested the seventh day, so must also we: and consequently, as hee spent six dayes in the worke of creation, so should wee in our personall callings. And S. *Paul* giveth this rule, *Eph. 4.28. Let him that stole steale no more, but let him rather worke with his hands the thing that is good, that hee may have to give to him that needeth.* Christ the head of men, lived with *Joseph* in the calling of a Carpenter, till the time of his baptisme, and hereupon it was that the Jewes said, *Is not this the carpenter the sonne of Mary?* and after he was baptized, and was as it were solemnly admitted into the office of a Mediatour, the worke of our redemption was then his calling, in which he both lived and died. Yea the Angels of God have their particular callings, in that they doe his *commandements in obeying the voyce of his word*. And therefore all that descend of *Adam* must needes have some calling to walke in, either publike, or private, whether it be in the Church, or Commonwealth, or family.

Hence we may learne sundry points of instruction; first of all, that it is a foule disorder in any Common-wealth, that there should bee suffered rogues, beggars, vagabonds; for such kind of persons commonly are of no civill societie or corporation, nor of any particular Church: and are as rotten legges, and armes that drop from the body. Againe, to wander up and downe from yeere to yeere to this end, to seeke and procure bodily maintenance, is no calling, but the life of a beast: and consequently a condition or state of life flat against the rule; That every one must have a particular calling. And therefore the Statute made the last Parliament for the restraining of beggars and rogues, is an excellent Statute, and being in substance the very law of God, is never to be repealed.

Againe, hereby is otherthrowen the condition of Monkes and Friars: who challenge to themselves that they live in a state of perfection, because they live apart from the societies of men in fasting and prayer: but contrariwise, this Monkish kind of living is damnable; for besides the generall duties of fasting and praier, which appertaine to al Christians, every man must have a particular & personal calling, that he may bee a good and profitable member of some society and body. And the auncient Church condemned all Monkes for theeves and robbers, that besides the generall duties of prayer and fasting, did not withal imploy themselves in some other calling for their better maintenance.

Thirdly, we learne by this, that miserable and damnable is the estate of those that beeing enriched with great livings and revenewes, do spend their daies in eating and drinking, in sports and pastimes, not imploying themselves in service for Church or Common-wealth. It may be haply thought, that such gentlemen have happy lives; but it is farre otherwise: considering every one, rich or poore, man or woman, is bound to have a personall calling, in which they must performe some duties for the common good, according to the measure of the gifts that God hath bestowed upon them.

Fourthly, hereby also it is required that such as we commonly call serving men, should have, beside the office of waiting, some other particular calling, unlesse they tend on men of great place and state: for onely to waite, and give attendance, is not a sufficient calling, as common experience telleth: for waiting servants, by reason they spend the most of their time in eating and drinking, sleeping and gaming after dinner and after supper, do proove the most unprofitable members both in Church and Common-wealth. For when either their good masters die, or they be turned out of their office for some misdemeanour, they are fit for no calling, being unable to labour; and thus they give themselves either to begge or steale.

The theory and practice of calling did not always mesh in colonial New England, as two Puritan fathers discovered to their dismay. The first, Ebenezer Parkman, the minister of Westborough, recorded his impressions in his diary (Proceedings of the American Antiquarian Society, vols. 71-73, 1961-63), as did Samuel Sewall (1652-1730), a Boston judge who touched New England life at nearly every point (Collections of the Massachusetts Historical Society, fifth series, vol. 5).

1726: 20 January. [When the Rev. Parkman went to Boston to see his sick father] Captain [Rowland] Storey convers'd with me about his Sons living with me . . . "Take the Lad, Sir, Till about May, when I expect to return from Sea, but if it please God to prevent me, if you like the Boy keep him till he is 15 or 16 years old, when I would have him put to apprentice. All I desire is that you keep him warm, and feed him Suitably. Instruct him in Christianity. My main Expectation and hope is that you'll give him Education proper to such an One. Let him Serve you as he is able, impose not on him those heavy burthens that will either Cripple him or Spoil his Growth. But in all regards I am willing he should Serve you to his Utmost. Upon my Consenting to this he said he had no Hatt. Let him have one of yours, and if it should so happen that he doth not remain with you I'll pay for it.

1744: 5 April. [While in Boston the Rev. Parkman was] Endeavouring to obtain a good place to bind my son Thomme [born 3 July 1729] out a 'Prentice.

17 April. Tom left for Boston to begin apprenticeship with Joshua Emms, Goldsmith.

19 May. My son Thomme much out of Health and Mr. Emms discourag'd about him and would have me send for him home.

1 June. I was full of Concern about my Son Thomme, my hopes all

blasted respecting his living with Mr. Emms, who is discourage'd and throws up [his hands]. I sought to Mr. Skelling the Carver, but in vain—to Mr. Samuel Jarvis, but not direct Success.

1745: 9 February. Mr. Joseph Batchellor [a weaver] of Grafton here, Who agreed to take my Son Thomme a Prentice next April.

27 March. Din'd at Mr. Joseph Knowltons: with whom I agreed to take his Son Nathan (who is about 11 Years of Age) for a Twelve Month, feeding, Clothing and instructing him.

15 April. My Son Thomas went to Live with Mr. Joseph Batchelour of Grafton, Weaver.

16 May. Thomme came home ill from Mr. Batchellors.

8 June. Thomme return'd to his Master Batchellor at Grafton.

15 June. Thomme return'd home again from Grafton being in such Pain and under So great Discouragement that his master sends all his Things Home with him. God grant the Grace and Wisdom needed under every Trial!

11 June. I have discover'd that though Ebenezer [his eldest son, born 20 August 1727] performs his Tasks of Lessons, yet he has in inward heavyness and drops now and then a word how glad he Shall be to be at Work upon the place, how much better the place Should Soon be if he Should labour etc. I therefore took the Opportunity this Morning to talk with him, and I once More still gave him Liberty to Choose what Method of Life Should Suit his Genius best.

13 June. Ebenezer discovers by all his Conduct that he preferrs Labour to Studying—and tho it grievously wounds me, yet I yield the point finally.

1747: 6 March. Thomme accompany'd by Ebenezer rode down to Marlborough to live at Mr. Williams's, the Sadler. May God be pleas'd to Smile on this attempt for his Benefit! and make him serviceable in his Generation!

1695: 19 February. Samuel [the eldest son of Samuel Sewall, born 11 June 1678] to be disposed to such a Master and Calling, as wherein he may abide with God.

15 July. I discourse with Capt. Saml. Checkly about his taking Sam. to be his Prentice. He seems to incline to it . . . The good Lord direct and prosper.

1696: 7 February. Last night Sam. could not sleep because of my Brother's speaking to him of removing to some other place, mentioning Mr. Usher's. . . . He mention'd to me Mr. Wadsworth's Sermon against Idleness, which was an Affliction to him. He said his was an idle Calling, and that he did more at home than there, take one day with another. And he mention'd Mr. Stoddard's words to me, that should place him with a good Master, and where had fullness of Imployment. It seems Sam. overheard him, and now alleged these words against his being where he was because of his idleness. Mention'd also the difficulty of the imployment by reason of the numerousness of Goods and hard to distinguish them, many not being marked; whereas Books, the price of them was set down, and so could sell them readily. I spake to Capt. Checkly again and again, and he gave me no encouragement that his being there would be to Sam's profit; and Mrs. Checkly always discouraging.

1697: 8 April. In the Morning agreed with Mr. Wilkins [a Boston bookseller] about Sam's living with him.

12 April. Sam. begins to go to Mr. Wilkins; Sold some of the Joy of Faith and some of Dr. Goodwin's 3d volum. At night we read Gal. 6.9.—in due season we shall reap, if we faint not. Lord furnish father and Son with Faith.

After finding a suitable master who agreed to take an apprentice, the parents drew up a legal agreement to be signed by the master and parents which stipulated the conditions and duties on both sides. The following indenture is a printed form found in the Massachusetts Historical Society.

This Indenture Witnesseth, That *Swain Lawton of the District of Pepperill in the County of Middlesex, a minor* Hath put *him*self, and by these Presents doth voluntarily, and of *his* own free Will and Accord, and with the Consent of *his Father Thomas Lawton of Pepperill afors: Housewright* put and bind *him*self Apprentice to *Jonas Wright of Pepperill aforesaid, Cordwainer*, to learn *his* Art, Trade or Mystery, and with *him* after the Manner of an Apprentice, to serve from the *Date hereof untill he shall arrive to Twenty years of age*, to be compleat and ended: During all which Term, the said Apprentice *the* said *Master* faithfully shall Serve, *his* Secrets keep, and Lawful Command every where gladly obey. *He* shall do no Damage to *his* said *Master* nor suffer it to be done by others, without letting, or giving Notice thereof to *his* said Master, shall not waste the Goods of *his* said *Master* nor Lend them Unlawfully to any. *He* shall not commit Fornication, nor Matrimony contract within the said Term. At Cards, Dice, or any other unlawful Game *he* shall not play: *he* shall not absent *him*self by Day or by Night from the Service of *his* said *Master* without *his* Leave; nor haunt Ale-Houses, Taverns, or Play Houses; but in all Things behave *him*self as a faithful Apprentice ought to do towards *his* said *Master* during the said Term.

And the said *Jonas Wright* for *him*self doth hereby Covenant and Promise to Teach and Instruct, or cause the said Apprentice to be taught and instructed in the Art, Trade or Calling of a *Cordwainer* by the best Way or Means *he* may or can (if the said Apprentice be capable to Learn) And to find and provide unto the said Apprentice good and sufficient *Meat, Drinke, Washing, Lodging, Physicke & Surgery in Case of Sickness or Lameness* during the said Term: And at the Expiration thereof to give unto the said Apprentice *Two good suits of apparril for all parts of his body, one suitable for Lords Days* & other Publick Occations, the other for every Days & to write a *Legiable hand* & Cypher as far as the Rule of three & to Read the *English Bible*.

In Testimony whereof the Parties to these Presents have hereunto Interchangeably set their Hand and seals the *31st* Day of *March* In the *Second* Year of the Reign of our Soverign Lord [*3 George*] of Great Britain, &c. Annoque Domini, One Thousand Seven Hundred and Sixty *Two*.

Since apprenticeship was so integral a part of the New England economic system, the colonial governments took pains to regulate its operation, as the following Massachusetts law of 1672 makes clear. It is taken from W.H. Whitmore's edition of The Colonial Laws of Massachusetts *(Boston, 1889), pp. 174-175.*

MASTERS, SERVANTS, LABOURERS.

It is Ordered by this Court and the Authority thereof. That no servant either Man or Mayd shall either give, Sell, or truck, any Commodity whatsoever, without Licence from their Masters, during the time of their service under pain of fine or corporal punishment at the discretion of the Court as the Offence shall deserve.

2. And that all Workmen shall worke the whole day, allowing convenient time for food and rest.

3. It is also Ordered that when any Servants shall run from their Masters or any other Inhabitants shall Privily go away, with suspicion of evill intentions, it shall be lawfull for the next Magistrate or the Constable and two of the cheife inhabitants, where no Magistrate is, to press men, and Boates or Pinnaces at the publick charge, to pursue such Persons by Sea and Land, and bring them back by force of Armes.

4. It is also Ordered by the authority aforesaid. That the freemen of every Town may from time to time as occasion shall require, agree among themselves about the prizes and rates of all workmens Labour and servants wages. And every person Inhabiting in any Towne, whether Workmen, Labourer or servant shall be bound to the same rates, which the said freemen, or the greater part shall bind themselves unto, and whosoever shall exceed those rates, so agreed, shall be punished by the discretion of the Court of that shire, according to the quality and measure of the Offence; And if any Town shall have Cause of Complaint against the freemen of any other Town, for allowing greater Rates or wages then themselves, the County Court of that shire, shall from Time to Time set Order therein.

5. *And for servants and workmens wages*, It is Ordered, that they may be payd in Corne to be valued by two indifferent freemen, chosen, the one by the Master, the other by the Servant or workman, who also are to have respect, to the value of the work or service, and if they cannot agree, then a third man shall be chosen by the next Magistrate, or if no Magistrate be in the Town, then by the next Constable, unles the parties agree the price themselves. Provided if any servant or workmen agree for any particular paiment, then to be payd in specie or consideration for default therein, And for all other paiments in Corn, if the parties cannot agree, they shall chose two indifferent men, & if they cannot agree, then a third as before.

6. It is Ordered, and by this Court Declared, That if any Servant shall flee from the tiranny and cruelty, of his or her Master, to the house of any freeman of the same Town, they shall be there protected and susteined till due order be taken for their relief; Provided due notice thereof be speedily given to their master from whom they fled; and to the next Magistrate or Constable where the party so fled is harboured.

7. Also that no servant shall be put off for above a year to any other, neither in the life of their Master, nor after their death by their

executors or administrators, unles it be by consent of Authority assembled in some Court, or two Assistants, otherwise all, and every such assignement to be voyd in Law.

8. And if any man smite out the eye or Tooth of his Man-servant or Mayd-servant, or otherwise Maim or much disfigure them (unles it be by meer casualty) he shall let them go free from his service, and shall allow such further recompencc as the Court shall adjudg him.

9. And all servants that have served diligently and faithfully to the benefit of their masters, Seven yeares, shall not be sent away empty; and if any have been unfaithfull, negligent or unprofitable in their service, notwithstanding the good usage of their masters, they shall not be dismissed, till they have made satisfaction according to the judgement of Authority. [1630, 33, 35, 36, 41]

Laws are seldom unbroken, and the delicate relationship between a master and his apprentice was subject to stress and strain. The following court actions reveal the depths to which some masters could go in the treatment of their charges. They are taken from the Records of the Colony of New Plymouth in New England *(Boston, 1855-61), vol. 3, pp. 71-73, 82, and the* Records and Files of the Quarterly Courts of Essex County Massachusetts *(Salem, 1911-21), vol. 8, pp. 91-92.*

* Att a Court of Assistants holden att Plymouth the sixt of Febrewary, 1654.

Before William Bradford, gentlē, Gou,   John Alden, and
            Willam Collyare,   Thomas Willett,
            Miles Standish,
                        Gentlemen, Asistants, &c.

The following verdict was ordered to bee recorded:—

Marshfeild, the last of January, 1654.

Wee, whose names are underwritten, being appointed a jury by Mr John Alden to view the dead body of John Walker, servant to Robert

Latham, of this towne, and to find the cause how hee came to his untimely end,—

Wee, upon due serch and examination, doe find that the body of John Walker was blackish and blew, and the skine broken in divers places from the middle to the haire of his head, viz , all his backe with stripes given him by his master, Robert Latham, as Robert himselfe did testify; and alsoe wee found a bruise of his left arme, and one of his left hipp, and one great bruise of his brest; and there was the knuckles of one hand and one of his fingers frozen, and alsoe both his heeles frozen, and one of the heeles the flesh was much broken, and alsoe one of his little toes frozen and very much perished, and one of his great toes frozen, and alsoe the side of his foot frozen; and alsoe, upon the reviewing the body, wee found three gaules like holes in the hames, which wee formerly, the body being frozen, thought they had been holes; and alsoe wee find that the said John was forced to carry a logg which was beyond his strength, which hee indeavoring to doe, the logg fell upon him, and hee, being downe, had a stripe or two, as Josepth Beedle doth testify; and wee find that it was some few daies before his death; and wee find, by the testimony of John Howland and John Adams, that heard Robert Latham say that hee gave John Walker som stripes that morning before his death; and alsoe wee find the flesh much broken of the knees of John Walker, and that hee did want sufficient food and cloathing and lodging, and that the said John did constantly wett his bedd and his cloathes, lying in them, and soe suffered by it, his clothes being frozen about him; and that the said John was put forth in the extremity of cold, though thuse unabled by lamenes and sorenes to pforme what was required; and therfore in respect of crewelty and hard usuage hee died; and alsoe, upon the 2cond review, the dead corpes did bleed att the nose.

> ARTHER HOWLAND,
> JOHN BRADFORD,
> JOSEPTH BEEDLE,
> ROBERT R C CARUER,
> JOHN DINGLEY,
> ANTHONY SNOW,
> JOHN BOURNE,
> JOHN HOWLAND, Junir,

JOHN THOMAS,
JOHN WALKER,
TIMOTHY WILLIAMS, his marke.
JOSEPH ROSE, his marke.

*Att the said Court the said Robert Latham appeered, and was ex-
amined, and after examination committed to the custidy of the cheife
marshall, and soe to remaine untill the next Generall Court, to bee
holden att New Plymouth the sixt of March, 1654, unlesse two sufficient men shall come in in the interim, and bee bound for his ap-
peerance, body for body.

*Att the Generall Court holden att New Plymouth the sixt Day of
March, 1654.

Before Willam Bradford, gent, Gou,   Timothy Hatherly,
         Willam Collyare,   John Browne,
         Thomas Prence,   John Alden, and
         Myles Standish,   Thomas Willett,
                    Gentlemen, Asistants, & c.

Robert Latham was indited for fellonious crewelty done unto John
Walker, his servant, aged about 14 yeares, by unreasonable correction, by withholding nessesary food and clothing, and by exposing his
said servant to extremitie of seasons, wherof the said John Walker
languished and imeadiately died, the 15 day of January, anno 1654.

The said Robert Latham put himselfe upon tryall, according to
law.

The grand jury found the bill of inditment a true bill.

Wherupon a pettye jury was impannelld and sent forth upon the
case; theire names are as followeth:—

Mr Thomas Dexter, Seni,
Josepth Andrews,
Robert Studson,
James Torrey,
Marke Eames,
Willam Paybody,
Robert Dennis,
Samuell Arnold,

Thomas Hinckley,
Nathaniell Bacon,
John Finney,
Richard Chadwell,
sworne

These found the said Robert Latham guilty of manslaughter by chaunc medley.

Wherupon the prisoner desired the benifitt of law, viz , a psalue of mercye, which was graunted him; and sentance was further pronownsed against him, which was, that the said Robert Latham should bee burned in the hand, and his haveing noe lands, that all his goods are confiscate unto his highnes the Lord Protector; and that the said sentance should bee forthwith executed; which accordingly was performed the 4th of March, 1654.

1681: March.

In the case of John Simmons and his servant, Thomas Bettis, court ordered that the servant return home with his master and recompense him for the damage sustained by his running away. Bettis was to serve him six months more than his time, and Simmons was advised moderation in the usage of his servant, and if he could agree with some other suitable person, to dispose of said servant.*

*Warrant, dated Mar. 17, 1680, from Nath. Saltonstall, assistant, to the prison keeper at Ipswich to receive Thomas Bettys, and to the constable of Bradford to deliver him.

Benjamin Kemball, aged forty-five years, deposed that a year ago last winter Thomas Bettys came to his house in the evening and stood outside the door. It was raining very hard and deponent asked him his business, but he answered hardly at all, so he bade him go home with one of Goodman West's boys. The next morning deponent, finding him in his barn quaking with cold, in mercy to a rational creature asked him into the house to warm himself. He wore very thin clothes, not suitable for the season.

Bill of cost of Nathan Webstor, constable of Bradford, who went three miles to seek Thomas Bettis, etc., 10s. Samuel Hart was bound for said Bettis' appearance at the next Ipswich court. Sworn, Mar. 18, 1680, before Daniel Denison.

Thomas Bettis' declaration: "my master haith this mani yeares beaten me upon small or frivelouse ocasion I have indevored to please and give my master content but I seldom can: he brocke my hed twice, strucke me one the hed wth a great stick: wch stick was tow long to strike me in the house for the flore: he brocke it upon his knees and then he strok me one the hed and stounded me I fell downe against the wall: the blood ran downe all my cloths to my feett my master tooke me up and washed of the blood wth a pigin of watter he feched sum suger and bound it up wth a cloth I was so disie all day that I cold nethr well se: or stand up right: my Arme wos so sore wth beating me att the same time that it was all black and blew: I cold not lift it up to my hed: yett my master wold have me goe to worke as sune as I cold and becase he had so beat me that I cold not keepe up wth my cumpani as I used to doe: my master told me that I was a hypokritte: after this I was abused sevarall times by him: one time he tied me to a beds foott: another time to a table foott: and also to a cradell foott and every time beate me cruely: and I was almost starved for want of cloth in the winter season in spesall when I stood in most need of cloths my first dame wold allwaise diswade my master and prayed him not to beate me: but this dame sets him one: I have bin so abused that I am afraid to live wth him ani more or ani longer and if your honars please to order me to live wth ani other master I am willing, but not to live wth him.''

John Boynton, aged about thirty years, deposed. Sworn, 25: 1: 1681, before N. Saltonstall, assistant.

Shu. Walker, aged about forty-two years, deposed that he lived near John Simmons and Bettes was a very naughty boy, etc. Sworn, 23: 1: 1681, before N. Saltonstall, assistant.

Samuell Emarson, aged about seventeen years, deposed that he had lived with his master Simmons about four years and Bettis was very rude in the family whenever his master was away, etc. Sworn, 25: 1: 1681, before N. Saltonstall, assistant.

Martin Forde, aged about twenty years, deposed that he heard Betts say that his master allowed him enough to eat and drink, etc. Sworn, 5: 1: 1681, before N. Saltonstall, assistant.

Nathan Webster, aged thirty-five years, deposed that in winter Betteys came to my house without any hat and very thinly clothed, etc. Sworn in court.

John Grant, aged about twenty-two years, deposed that living at Simmons' house, he had seen the latter beat Bettys so that he fainted. Also that at one time he tied him to a cradle, having pulled off all his clothes to his shirt, and whipped him with three cords tied to a stick so that he brought blood, while he asked the boy if he loved him. The boy said yes and he beat him again. At another time, when the boy was going out to wkr, Simons called him in and bade him blow the fire, etc. Sworn in court.

Life in New England even in the earliest years, was not all work. The only two contemporary accounts of the first thanksgiving show why. The first is from William Bradford, Of Plymouth Plantation 1620-1641, *ed. Samuel Eliot Morison (New York, 1952), p. 90; the second from Edward Winslow's letter dated Tuesday, 11 December 1621, printed in the* Chronicles of the Pilgrim Fathers, *ed. Alexander Young (Boston, 1841), pp. 60-65.*

They began now [sometime after 18 September 1621, the date of the previous entry] to gather in the small harvest they had, and to fit up their houses and dwellings against winter, being all well recovered in health and strength and had all things in good plenty. For as some were thus employed in affairs abroad, others were exercised in fishing, about cod and bass and other fish, of which they took good store, of which every family had their portion. All the summer there was no want; and now began to come in store of fowl, as winter approached, of which this place did abound when they came first (but afterward decreased by degrees). And besides waterfowl there was great store of wild turkeys, of which they took many, besides venison, etc. Besides they had about a peck a meal a week to a person, or now since harvest, Indian corn to that proportion. Which made many afterwards write so largely of their plenty here to their friends in England, which were not feigned but true reports.

We set the last Spring some twentie Acres of *Indian* Corne, and sowed some six Acres of Barly & Pease, and according to the manner of the *Indians,* we manured our ground with Herings or rather Shadds, which we have in great abundance, and take with great ease at our doores. Our Corne did prove well, & God be praysed, we had a good increase of *Indian*-Corne, and our Barly indifferent good, but our Pease not worth the gathering, for we feared they were too late sowne, they came up very well, and blossomed, but the Sunne parched them in the blossome; our harvest being gotten in, our Governour sent foure men on fowling, that so we might after a more speciall manner rejoyce together, after we had gathered the fruit of our labours; they foure in one day killed as much fowle, as with a little helpe beside, served the Company almost a weeke, at which time amongst other Recreations, we exercised our Armes, many of the *Indians* coming amongst us, and amongst the rest their greatest King *Massasoyt*, with some ninetie men, whom for three dayes we entertained and feasted, and they went out and killed five Deere, which they brought to the Plantation and bestowed on our Governour, and upon the Captaine, and others. And although it be not alwayes so plentifull, as it was at this time with us, yet by the goodnesse of God, we are so farre from want, that we often wish you partakers of our plentie.

The Puritans obviously enjoyed other forms of recreation, as the Massachusetts laws of 1672 reveal at some length. One of those forms, dancing, won the special attention of the orthodox clergy in the form of a pamphlet entitled An Arrow against Profane and Promiscuous Dancing. Drawn out of a Quiver of the Scriptures *(Boston, 1684) by the Rev. Increase Mather. The excerpts which follow come from pp. 1-3, 27-30; the laws are taken from W.H. Whitmore's edition of* The Colonial Laws of Massachusetts *(Boston, 1889), pp. 163-166.*

INKEEPERS, ORDINARIES, TIPLING, DRUNKENNES.

For as much as there is a necessary use of houses of Common— entertainment, in every Common wealth and of such as retaile wine, beer, and victuals, yet because there are so many abuses, both by persons entertaining, and by persons entertained, It is therefore Ordered by this Court and Authority thereof, That no person or persons shall at any time, under any pretence or Colour whatsoever, undertake to be a Common victualer, keeper of a Cooks shop, or house for Common entertainment, Taverner or publick seller of wine, Ale, beer or strong-waters, by retaile, (nor shall any sell wine privately in his house, or out of doores, by a less quantity then a quarter caske) without approbation of the Selected Townsmen, and License of the County Court, where they dwell, upon pain of forefeiture of *five pounds*, for every such offence; or imprisonment at the pleasure of the Court. Provided it shall be Lawfull for any whole-sale Merchant

of wines, or the present Stillers of strong waters, being Masters of
families, or such as receive the same, from Forraine parts, in cases
&c. or makers of Cyder, to sell by retaile; Provided the quantity of
wine and cyder, be not less then three gallons at a time, to one person, nor strong waters less then a quart; and that it be only to masters
of families of good and honest report, or persons going to Sea, and
they suffer not any person to drink the same in their houses, cellars
or yards.

And every Person so Licensed, for common entertainment, shall
have some inoffensive Sign, obvious, for direction of Strangers, and
such as have no such sign, after three months so Licensed, shall loose
their license, and others be allowed in their stead.

2. And every person Licensed to keep an Ordinary, shall
allwayes be provided of strong wholesome Beer, of four bushels of
Mault (at the least) to a hogshead, which he shall not sell at above
two-pence the Ale-quart, upon penalty of *Fourty shillings* for the
first offence, and for the second offence to loose his License.

And it is permitted to any that will, to sell beer out of dores, at one
penny the ale-quart, or under.

3. And no Licensed person as aforesaid, shall suffer any to be
drunke, or to drinke excessively, *viz.* above halfe a pint of wine for
one person, at a time, or to continue Tipling, above the space of halfe
an hour, or at unseasonable times, or after nine of the Clock at night,
in, or about any of their houses, on penalty of *five shillings* for every
such Offence.

And if any person Licenced to sell wine or Beer as aforesayd, shall
Conceale in his house any person that shall be found Drunken, and
shall not forthwith procure a Constable to carry such Drunken person, before some Magistrate or Commissioner; and in the interim,
the said Wintner or drawer of beer, shall make stay of such persons,
till the Constable shall come, under the penalty of *Five Pounds*, for
every default.

4. And every person found Drunken. *viz.* so as he be thereby
bereaved or disabled in the use of his understanding, appearing in
his speech or gesture, in any of the said houses or elswhere, shall
forfeit, *ten shillings*, and for excessive Drinking *three shillings foure
pence*, and for continueing above half an houre tipling, *two shillings
six pence*, and for tipling at unseasonable times, or after nine of the
clock at night, *five shillings* for every Offence in those particulars,

being Lawfully convict thereof, and for want of paiment they shall be imprisoned til they pay, or be set in the Stocks one hour or more, (in some open place) as the weather will permit not exceeding three houres.

5. And if any person be found drunken, by night or by day, or shall in his drunkenness offer any abuse to the Constable or others, either by striking, or reviling him or them, or using any endeavours, by himselfe or others, to make an escape, it shall be in the power of the Constable, to commit such person or persons, to safe keeping or imprisonment, or take bond for his appearance, as he shall see cause; and the keepers of each prison, upon Warrant from any Magistrate, or Commissioner or Select men, shall receive all such as shall be so committed, and take but *twelve pence* for his fee in such cases . . .

6. It shall be Lawfull notwithstanding, for all licensed persons to entertain land-travellors, or sea-faring men, in the night season, when they come on shore, or from their journey, for their necessary refreshment, or when they prepare for their voyage or journey the next day early, so there be no disorder among them; and also strangers, lodgers, or other persons, in an orderly way, may continue in such houses of common entertainment during meale times, or upon lawfull busines, what time their occasions shall require. . . .

8. And if any person offend in drunkennes, excessive or long drinking, the second time, they shall pay double fines. And if they fall into the same offence the third time, they shall pay treble the fines; & if the parties be not able to pay the fines, then he that is found drunke, shall be punished by whipping, to the number of *ten stripes*, and he that offends in excessive or long drinking, shall be put into the stocks, for three houres, when the weather may not hazzard his life or limbs. And if they offend the fourth time, they shall be imprisoned, untill they put in two sufficient suretyes for their good behaviour. . . .

10. It is further Ordered, that every Inkeeper or victualler, shall provide for the entertainment of strangers hourses, *viz.* one or more inclosures, for summer, hay and Provender for winter, with convenient stable-roome and attendance, under the penalty of *two shillings six pence* for every dayes default, & double damage to the party thereby wronged, except it be by inevitable accident. . . .

12. And it is Ordered. That in all places where week day Lectures are kept, All Taverners, Victuallers and Ordinaries, that are within

one Mile of the Meeting-house to which they belong, shall from time to time, Cleer their houses of all persons able to go to meeting, during the time of the exercise, (except upon extraordinary cause, for the necessary refreshing of strangers unexpectedly repairing to them) upon paine of five *shillings* for every such Offence over and besides the penalties incurred by this Law for any other Disorder. . . .

14. It is further Ordered by the Authority aforesayd. That all Constables may, and shall from time to time, duely make search, throughout the limits of their Townes upon Lords Dayes and Lecture dayes in times of exercise, and also at all other times so oft as they shall see cause for all Offences and Offenders against this Law, in any the particulars thereof. . . .

GAMING & DANCING.

Upon Complaint of the disorders, by the use of the Games of shuffle-board and Bowling, in and about houses of common entertainment, whereby much precious time is spent unprofitably, & much *wast of wine and beer occasioned*; It is Ordered by this Court and the Authority thereof, That no Person shall henceforth, use the said Games of shufle-board or bowling, or any other play or game, in, or about any such house, nor in any other house used as Common for such purpose, upon paine for every keeper of such house, to forfeit for every such Offence *Five Shillings*. Nor shall any person at any time, play or Game for any mony, or mony worth, upon penalty of forfeiting treble the Value thereof, one halfe to the party informing and the other halfe to the Treasury, nor shall any person be an Abettor to any kind of gaming on the like penaltie. Nor shall there be any dauncing in ordinaries upon any occasion, on the penaltie of *five shillings* for every person that shall offend: and any Magistrate may hear & determine any offence against this Law. [1646, 47, 51.]

For preventing disorders arising in several places within this Jurisdiction; by reason of some still observing such feastivals, as were superstitiously kept in other Countryes, to the Great dishonour of God and Offence of others. It is therefore Ordered by this Court and Authority thereof. That whosoever shall be found observing any such day, as Christmas or the like, either by forbearing labour, feasting, or any other way upon any such account as aforesayd, every such person so offending, shall pay for every such Offence *Five shillings*, as a fine to the County. *And whereas not onely at such times but severall other times also, it is a Custome too frequent in many places to expend time in unlawfull Games, as Cards, Dice* &c. It is therefore further Ordered and by this Court declared. That after publication hereof whosoever shall be found in any place within this Jurisdiction playing either at cards or at dice. Contrary to this Order, shall pay as a fine to the County the sum of *Five Shillings* for every such Offence.

AN ARROW AGAINST PROFANE AND PROMISCUOUS DANCING

Concerning the Controversy about *Dancing*, the Question is not, whether all *Dancing* be in it self sinful. It is granted, that *Pyrrhical* or *Polemical Saltation:* i.e. when men vault in their Armour, to shew their strength and activity, may be of use. Nor is the question, whether a sober and grave *Dancing* of Men with Men, or of Women with Women, be not allowable; we make no doubt of that, where it may be done without offence, in due season, and with moderation. The Prince of Philosophers has observed truly, that *Dancing* or *Leaping*, is a natural expression of joy: So that there is no more Sin in it, than in laughter, or any outward expression of inward Rejoycing.

But our question is concerning *Gynecandrical Dancing*, or that which is commonly called *Mixt* or *Promiscuous Dancing, viz.* of Men and Women (be they elder or young persons) together: Now this we affirm to be utterly unlawful, and that it cannot be tollerated in such a place as *New-England*, without great Sin. And that it may appear, that we are not transported by Affection without Judgment, let the following Arguments be weighed in the Ballance of the Sanctuary.

Arg. I. *That which the Scripture condemns is sinful*. None but Atheists will deny this *Proposition:* But the Scripture condemns *Promiscuous Dancing*. This *Assumption* is proved, I. *From the Seventh Commandment*. It is an Eternal Truth to be observed in expounding the Commandments, that whenever any sin is forbidden, not only the highest acts of that sin, but all degrees thereof, and all occasions leading thereto are prohibited. Now we cannot find one Orthodox and Judicious Divine, that writeth on the Commandments, but mentions *Promiscuous Dancing*, as a breach of the seventh Commandment, as being an occasion, and an incentive to that which is evil in the sight of God. Yea, this is so manifest as that the *Assembly* in the *larger Catechism*, do expresly take notice of *Dancings*, as a violation of the Commandments. It is sad, that when in times of Reformation, Children have been taught in their C[a]techism, that such *Dancing* is against the Commandment of God, that now in *New-England* they should practically be learned the contrary. The unchast Touches and Gesticulations used by *Dancers*, have a palpable tendency to that which is evil. Whereas some object, that they are not sensible of any ill motions occasioned in them, by being Spectators or Actors in such *Saltations;* we are not bound to believe all which some pretend concerning their own Mortification. . . .

Now they that frequent Promiscuous Dancings, or that send their Children thereunto, walk disorderly, and contrary to the Apostles Doctrine. It has been proved that such a practice is a *Scandalous Immorality*, and therefore to be removed out of Churches by Discipline, which is the Broom of Christ, whereby he keeps his Churches clean . . .

And shall Churches in *N[ew] E[ngland]* who have had a Name to be stricter and purer than other Churches, suffer such a scandalous evil amongst them? if all that are under Discipline be made sensible of this matter, we shall not be much or long infested with a *Choreutical Daemon*. . . .

The Catechism which Wicked men teach their Children is to Dance and to Sing. Not that Dancing, or Musick, or Singing are in themselves sinful: but if the Dancing Master be wicked they are commonly abused to lasciviousness, and that makes them to become abominable. But will you that are Professors of Religion have your Children to be thus taught? the Lord expects that you should give the Children who are Baptized into his Name another kind of Education, that you should bring them up in the nurture and admonition of the Lord: And do you not hear the Lord Expostulating the case with you, and saying, you have taken my Children, the Children that were given unto me; the Children that were solemnly engaged to renounce the Pomps of Satan; but is this a light matter that you have taken these my Children, and initiated them in the Pomps and Vanities of the Wicked one, contrary to your Covenant? What will you say in the day of the Lords pleading with you? we have that charity for you as to believe that you have erred through Ignorance, and not wickedly: and we have therefore accounted it our Duty to inform you in the Truth. If you resolve not on Reformation, you will be left inexcusable. However it shall be, we have now given our Testimony and delivered our own Souls. *Consider what we say, and the Lord give you understanding in all things.*

V. RIGHT AND WRONG

The Puritan conception of right and wrong was at once trivial and grand. Upon what testament of the Bible was it predominately based? Why were some Puritan laws so picayune? Why were some so harsh? What did the capital crimes have in common? What was New England's relationship with God? What kind of behavior did this require? Why? What were the enemies of the New England ideal? Who was welcome in New England? Were the Puritans tolerant? What was the limit of their toleration? Why were the Puritans concerned about fancy clothes and long hair? What defined ''excessive'' apparel? Who was exempt from the restrictions on dress? Why? With what undesireable persons did the Puritans associate the wearers of long hair? What were the religious objections to long hair? What would be the objections of the society envisioned by John Winthrop?

The most famous sermon in New England's history was given not by a minister but by Governor John Winthrop (1588-1649) of the Massachusetts Bay Company on board the Arbella *as it sailed toward New England in 1630. Winthrop's ''Modell of Christian Charity'' was a blueprint for the future colony that would unite in one unfailing bond religion and society. As such it laid down the broadest standards of law and conduct for the New Englishmen. The excerpts which follow come from the* Winthrop Papers *(Boston: Massachusetts Historical Society, 1929—), vol. 2, pp. 282-295.*

A MODELL OF CHRISTIAN CHARITY

Written
On Boarde the Arrabella,
On the Attlantick Ocean.
By the Honorable John Winthrop Esquire.

In His passage, (with the great Company of Religious people, of which Christian Tribes he was the Brave Leader and famous Governor;) from the Island of Great Brittaine, to New-England in the North America.

Anno 1630.

Christian Charitie.

A Modell Hereof.

God Almightie in his most holy and wise providence hath soe disposed of the Condicion of mankinde, as in all times some must be rich some poore, some highe and eminent in power and dignitie; others meane and in subieccion.

The Reason Hereof.

1. Reas: *First*, to hold conformity with the rest of his workes, being delighted to shewe forthe the glory of his wisdome in the variety and differance of the Creatures and the glory of his power, in ordering all these differences for the preservacion and good of the whole, and the glory of his greatnes that as it is the glory of princes to have many officers, soe this great King will have many Stewards counting himselfe more honoured in dispenceing his guifts to man by man, then if hee did it by his owne immediate hand.

2. Reas: *Secondly*, That he might have the more occasion to manifest the worke of his Spirit: first, upon the wicked in moderateing and restraineing them: soe that the riche and mighty should not eat upp the poore, nor the poore, and dispised rise upp against their superiours, and shake off theire yoake; 2ly in the regenerate in exerciseing his graces in them, as in the greate ones, theire love mercy, gentlenes, temperance etc., in the poore and inferiour sorte, theire faithe patience, obedience etc:

3. Reas: Thirdly, That every man might have need of other, and from hence they might be all knitt more nearly together in the Bond of brotherly affeccion: from hence it appeares plainely that noe man is made more honourable then another or more wealthy etc., out of any perticuler and singuler respect to himselfe but for the glory of his Creator and the Common good of the Creature, Man; Therefore God still reserves the propperty of these guifts to himselfe as Ezek: 16. 17. he there calls wealthe his gold and his silver etc. Prov: 3. 9. he claimes theire service as his due honour the Lord with thy riches etc. All men being thus (by divine providence) rancked into two sortes, riche and poore; under the first, are comprehended all such as are able to live comfortably by theire owne meanes duely improved; and all others are poore according to the former distribution. There are two rules whereby wee are to walke one towards another: JUSTICE and MERCY. These are allwayes distinguished in theire Act and in theire object, yet may they both concurre in the same Subject in eache respect; as sometimes there may be an occasion of shewing mercy to a rich man, in some sudden danger of distresse, and allsoe doeing of meere Justice to a poor man in regard of some perticuler contract etc. There is likewise a double Lawe by which wee are regulated in our conversacion one towardes another: in both the former respects, the lawe of nature and the lawe of grace, or the morrall lawe or the lawe of the gospell, to omitt the rule of Justice as not propperly belonging to this purpose otherwise then it may fall into consideracion in some perticuler Cases: By the first of these lawes man as he was enabled soe withall [is] commaunded to love his neighbour as himselfe upon this ground stands all the precepts of the morall lawe, which concernes our dealings with men. To apply this to the works of mercy this lawe requires two things first that every man afford his help to another in every want or distresse Secondly, That hee performe this out of the same affeccion, which makes him carefull of his owne good according to that of our Saviour Math: [7. 12.] Whatsoever ye would that men should doe to you. This was practised by Abraham and Lott in entertaineing the Angells and the old man of Gibea.

The Lawe of Grace or the Gospell hath some differance from the former as in these respectes first the lawe of nature was given to man in the estate of innocency; this of the gospell in the estate of regeneracy: 2ly, the former propounds one man to another, as the same fleshe and Image of god, this as a brother in Christ allsoe, and in the Communion of the same spirit and soe teacheth us to put a difference betweene Christians and others. Doe good to all especially to the household of faith; upon this ground the Israelites were to putt a difference betweene the brethren of such as were strangers though not of the Canaanites. 3ly. The Lawe of nature could give noe rules for dealeing with enemies for all are to be considered as freinds in the estate of innocency, but the Gospell commaunds love to an enemy. proofe[:] If thine Enemie hunger feede him; Love your Enemies doe good to them that hate you Math: 5. 44.

This Lawe of the Gospell propoundes likewise a difference of seasons and occasions there is a time when a christian must sell all and give to the poore as they did in the Apostles times. There is a tyme allsoe when a christian (though they give not all yet) must give beyond theire abillity, as they of Macedonia. Cor: 2. 6. likewise community of perills calls for extraordinary liberallity and soe doth Community in some speciall service for the Churche. Lastly, when there is noe other meanes whereby our Christian brother may be releived in this distresse, wee must help him beyond our ability, rather then tempt God, in putting him upon help by miraculous or extraordinary meanes. . . .

1. For the persons, wee are a Company professing our selves fellow members of Christ, In which respect onely though wee were absent from eache other many miles, and had our imploymentes as farre distant, yet wee ought to account our selves knitt together by this bond of love, and live in the exercise of it, if wee would have comforte of our being in Christ, this was notorious in the practise of the Christians in former times, as is testified of the Waldenses from the mouth of one of the adversaries Aeneas Syluius, mutuo [solent amare] penè antequam norint, they use to love any of their owne religion even before they were acquainted with them.

2ly. for the worke wee have in hand, it is by a mutuall consent through a speciall overruleing providence, and a more then an ordinary approbation of the Churches of Christ to seeke out a place of Cohabitation and Consorteshipp under a due forme of Government both civill and ecclesiasticall. In such cases as this the care of the publique must oversway all private respects, by which not onely conscience, but meare Civill pollicy doth binde us; for it is a true rule that perticuler estates cannott subsist in the ruine of the publique.

3ly. The end is to improve our lives to doe more service to the Lord the comforte and encrease of the body of christe whereof wee are members that our selves and posterity may be the better preserved from the Common corrupcions of this evill world to serve the Lord and worke out our Salvacion under the power and purity of his holy Ordinances.

4ly for the meanes whereby this must bee effected, they are 2fold, a Conformity with the worke and end wee aime at, these wee see are extraordinary, therefore wee must not content our selves with usuall ordinary meanes whatsoever wee did or ought to have done when wee lived in England, the same must wee doe and more allsoe where wee goe: That which the most in theire Churches maineteine as a truthe in profession onely, wee must bring into familiar and constant practice, as in this duty of love wee must love brotherly without dissimulation, wee must love one another with a pure hearte fervently wee must beare one anothers burthens, wee must not looke onely on our owne things, but allsoe on the things of our brethren, neither must wee think that the lord will beare with such faileings at our hands as hee dothe from those among whome wee have lived. . . .

Thus stands the cause betweene God and us, wee are entered into Covenant with him for this worke, wee haue taken out a Commission, the Lord hath given us leave to drawe our owne Articles wee have professed to enterprise these Accions upon these and these ends, wee haue hereupon besought him of favour and blessing: Now if the Lord shall please to heare us, and bring us in peace to the place wee desire, then hath hee ratified this Covenant and sealed our Commission, [and] will expect a strickt performance of the Articles contained in it, but if wee shall neglect the observacion of these Articles which are the ends wee have propounded, and dissembling with our God, shall fall to embrace this present world and prosecute our carnall intencions seekeing greate things for our selves and our posterity, the Lord will surely breake out in wrathe against us be revenged of such a perjured people and make us knowe the price of the breache of such a Covenant.

Now the onely way to avoyde this shipwracke and to provide for our posterity is to followe the Counsell of Micah, to doe Justly, to love mercy, to walke humbly with our God, for this end, wee must be knitt together in this worke as one man, wee must entertaine each other in brotherly Affeccion, wee must be willing to abridge our selves of our superfluities, for the supply of others necessities, wee must uphold a familiar Commerce together in all meekenes, gentlenes, patience and liberallity, wee must delight in eache other, make others Condicions our owne rejoyce together, mourne together, labour, and suffer together, allwayes haveing before our eyes our Commission and Community in the worke, our Community as members of the same body, soe shall wee keepe the unitie of the spirit in the bond of peace, the Lord will be our God and delight to dwell among us, as his owne people and will commaund a blessing upon us in all our wayes, soe that wee shall see much more of his wisdome power goodnes and truthe then formerly wee have been acquainted with, wee shall finde that the God of Israell is among us, when tenn of us shall be able to resist a thousand of our enemies, when hee shall make us a prayse and glory, that men shall say of succeeding plantacions: the lord make it like that of New England: for wee must Consider that wee shall be as a Citty upon a Hill, the eies of all people are uppon us; soe that if we shall deale falsely with our god in this worke wee have undertaken and soe cause him to withdrawe his present help from us, wee shall be made a story and a by-word through the world, wee shall open the mouthes of enemies to speake evill of the wayes of god and all professours for Gods sake; wee shall shame the faces of many of gods worthy servants, and cause theire prayers to be turned into Cursses upon us till wee be consumed out of the good land whether wee are goeing: And to shutt upp this discourse with that exhortacion of Moses that faithfull servant of the Lord in his last farewell to Irsaell Deut. 30. Beloved there is now sett before us life, and good, deathe and evill in that wee are Commaunded this day to love the Lord our God, and to love one another to walke in his wayes and to keepe his Commaundements and his Ordinance, and his lawes, and the Articles of our Covenant with him that wee may live and be multiplyed, and that the Lord our God may blesse us in the land whether wee goe to possesse it: But if our heartes shall turne away soe that wee will not obey, but shall be seduced and worshipp . . . other Gods our pleasures, and proffitts, and serve them; it is propounded unto us this day, wee shall surely perishe out of the good Land whether wee passe over this vast Sea to possesse it;

> Therefore lett us choose life,
> that wee, and our Seede,
> may live; by obeyeing his
> voyce, and cleaveing to him,
> for hee is our life, and
> our prosperity.

The things that people are willing to die—and to kill—for are sensitive indications of the character of those people. The capital laws of Massachusetts were first published in 1641 in the Body of Liberties, *the first legal code, accompanied by the Biblical references that warranted the extreme punishment. Nearly as indicative of the New England social character are its non-capital laws, two of which are given below. All the laws cited are taken from W.H. Whitmore's edition of* The Colonial Laws of Massachusetts *(Boston, 1889), pp. 55, 193-194.*

Capitall Laws

1.

Dut. 13. 6, 10.
Dut. 17. 2, 6.
Ex. 22. 20.

If any man after legall conviction shall have or worship any other god, but the lord god, he shall be put to death.

2.

Ex. 22. 18.
Lev. 20. 27.
Dut. 18. 10.

If any man or woeman be a witch, (that is hath or consulteth with a familiar spirit,) They shall be put to death.

3.

Lev. 24. 15, 16.

If any man shall Blaspheme the name of god, the father, Sonne or Holie ghost, with direct, expresse, presumptuous or high handed blasphemie, or shall curse god in the like manner, he shall be put to death.

4.

Ex. 21. 12.
Numb. 35. 13, 14, 30, 31.

If any person committ any wilfull murther, which is manslaughter, committed upon premeditated mallice, hatred, or Crueltie, not in a mans necessarie and just defence, nor by meere casualtie against his will, he shall be put to death.

5.

Numb. 25. 20, 21.
Lev. 24. 17.

If any person slayeth an other suddaienly in his anger or Crueltie of passion, he shall be put to death.

6.

Ex. 21. 14.

If any person shall slay an other through guile, either by poysening or other such divelish practice, he shall be put to death.

7.

Lev. 20. 15, 16.

If any man or woeman shall lye with any beaste or bruite creature by Carnall Copulation, They shall surely be put to death. And the beast shall be slaine and buried and not eaten.

8.

Lev. 20. 13.   If any man lyeth with mankinde as he lyeth with a woeman, both of them have committed abhomination, they both shall surely be put to death.

9.

Lev. 20. 19, and 18, 20. Dut. 22. 23, 24.   If any person committeth Adultery with a married or espoused wife, the Adulterer and Adulteresse shall surely be put to death.

10.

Ex. 21. 16.   If any man stealeth a man or mankinde, he shall surely be put to death.

11.

Deut. 19. 16, 18, 19.   If any man rise up by false witnes, wittingly and of purpose to take away any mans life, he shall be put to death.

12.

If any man shall conspire and attempt any invasion, insurrection, or publique rebellion against our commonwealth, or shall indeavour to surprize any Towne or Townes, fort or forts therein, or shall treacherously and perfedioustie attempt the alteration and subversion of our frame of politie or Government fundamentallie, he shall be put to death.

STRANGERS

Whereas we are credibly Informed, that great mischiefs have been done to other Plantations, by the resort of Commanders, Souldiers and other strangers, to prevent the like in this Jurisdiction, It is Ordered by this Court and Authority thereof, That henceforth all Strangers of what quality soever, above the age of *sixteen yeares,* arriving in any *Ports* or parts of this Jurisdiction, in any ship or vessel, shall immediately be brought before the Governour, Deputy Governour or two other Magistrates, by the Master or Mate of the said ship or vessel, upon penalty of *twenty pound* for default thereof, there to give an account of their occasions, and buisines in this Country, whereby satisfaction may be given, and order taken, with such strangers, as the said Governour, Deputy Governour, two Magistrates, or the next County Court shall see meet, who shall keep a Record of the names and qualities of all such strangers, to be Returned to the next Generall Court, *and for the publication of this Order.* It is Ordered the same be posted upon the doors or posts of the Meeting houses, & other publick places in all the port townes, of this Jurisdiction. And the Captain of the Castle, shall make known this Order to every Ship or Vessel as it passeth by, and the Constable of every port Town shall endeavour to do the like, to such ships and vessels before they Land their Passengers. [1651]

And if any strangers or people of other nations, professing the true Christian Religion, shall fly to us, from the tyranny or oppression of their persecutors, or from famine, warrs or the like necessary & Compulsory Cause, they shall be entertained & succoured amongst us according to that power & prudence God shall give us. [1641]

Every person within this Jurisdiction, whether Inhabitant or stranger, shall enjoy the same Law and Justice, that is generall for this Jurisdiction, which we constitute & execute one towards another in all Cases proper to our Cognizance without partiallity or delay. [1641]

No town or person shall receive any stranger Resorting hither with intent to Reside in this Jurisdiction, nor shall allow any Lot or Habitation to any or entertain any such above three Weeks, except such person shall have allowance, under the hand of some one Magistrate, upon Pain of every Town, that shall give or sell, any Lot or habitation, to any not so Licensed, such fine to the Country, as the County Court shall impose, not exceeding *fifty pound* nor less then *four pounds*, and for every month after so offending, shall forfeit as aforesaid, not exceeding *ten pounds*, nor less then *fourty shillings*, And every Constable shall enform the Courts, of all new commers, which they know to be admitted without License from time to time. [1637, 38, 47]

SWEARING & CURSING

It is Ordered by this Court & Authority thereof, That if any person within this Jurisdiction, shall *Swear rashly* & vainly, by the Holy *name of God*, or *other Oath*, he shall forfeit to the common Treasury for every such offence *ten shillings*, and it shall be in the power of any Magistrate by warrant to the Constable, to *call such person before him*, and upon sufficient proof, to *sentence such offender*, and to give order to *levy the fine*, and if such person be not able, or shall refuse to pay the said fine, he shall be *committed to the stocks*, there to continue not exceeding *three houres*, nor less then *one houre*.

2. And if any person shall *swear* more Oaths then *one at a time*, before he remove out of the room or company where he so sweares,

he shall then pay *twenty shillings*. The like penalty shall be inflicted
for *prophane and wicked Cursing*, of any person or creature, and for
the multiplying the same, as is appointed for *prophane swearing*, and
in case any person so offending, by *multiplying oaths* or *cursing*,
shall not pay his or their fines forthwith, they shall be *whipt* or *committed to prison*, till they shall pay the same, at the discretion of the
Court or Magistrate, that shall have Cognizance thereof.

*Sometimes seemingly trivial events reveal more about a society
than its more newsworthy wars, crimes, and achievements. In colonial New England the wearing of fancy clothing and long hair created
a furor that rivalled in intensity and duration the tonsorial tizzy of
the 1960s. The first two documents are Massachusetts General
Court actions designed to halt the excesses in fashions. They come
from the* Records of the Governor and Company of the Massachusetts Bay in New England *(Boston, 1853-54), vol. 1, pp. 126,
274.*

1634: 3 SEPTEMBER.

The Court, takeing into consideracõn the greate, supfluous, & unnecessary expences occacõned by reason of some newe & imodest
fashions, as also the ordinary weareing of silver, golde, & silke laces,
girdles, hatbands, &c, hath therefore ordered that noe pson, either
man or woman, shall hereafter make or buy any appẽll, either
wollen, silke, or lynnen, with any lace on it, silver, golde, silke, or
threed, under the penalty of forfecture of such cloathes, ℓð./
*Also, that noe pson, either man or woman, shall make or buy any
slashed cloathes, other then one slashe in each sleeve, and another in
the backe; also, all cuttworks, imbroidered or needle worke capps,
bands, & rayles, arc forbidden hereafter to be made & worne, under
the aforesaid penalty; also, all golde or silver girdles, hattbands,
belts, ruffs, beavr hatts, are prohibited to be bought & worne hereafter, under the aforesaid penalty, ℓð./
Moreover, it is agreed, if any man shall judge the weareing of any
the forenamed pticulars, newe fashions, or longe haire, or any thing
of the like nature, to be uncomely, or piudiciall to the comon good,
the pty offending reforme not the same upon notice given him, that
then the nexte Assistant, being informed thereof, shall have power to

binde the p̄ty soe offending to answer it att the nexte Court, if the case soe requires; próvided & it is the meaneing of the Court that men & women shall have liberty to weare out such app̄ell as they are nowe proveded of, (except the imoderate greate sleeues, slashed app̄ell, imoderate greate rayles, longe wings, ℰᶜ ;) this order to take place a fortnight after the publishing thereof.

1639: **9 SEPTEMBER.**

Whereas there is much complaint of the excessive wearing of lace, & other superfluities tending to little use or benefit, but to the nourishing of pride & exhausting of mens estates, & also of evill example to others, it is therefore ordered by this Court, & decreed, that henceforward no person whatsoever shall psume to buy or sell, wthin this jurisdiction, any manner of lace, to bee worne or used wthin our limits./

And that no taylor, or any other person whatsoever, shall hereafter set any lace or points upon any garments, either linnen, wollen, or any other wearing cloathes whatsoever, & that no pson hereafter shalbee imployed in making of any manner of lace, but such as they shall sell to such persons as shall & will transport the same out of this jurisdiction, who, in such case, shall have liberty to buy the same: And that hearafter no garment shalbee made wth short sleeves, whereby the nakedness of the arme may bee discovered in the wearing thereof; & such as have garments already made wth short sleeves shall not hereafter were the same, unless they cover their armes to the wrist wth linnen, or otherwise: And that hearafter no person whatsoever shall make any garment for weomen, or any of ther sex, wth sleeves more then halfe an elle wide in the widest place thereof, so proportionable for biger or smaller persons./

Ten years later the chief magistrates of Massachusetts gave notice of their dislike of the new fashion of long hair. The following copy was taken, significantly, from the records of Harvard College, home of the most flagrant "long-hairs". It is printed in the Publications of the Colonial Society of Massachusetts, *vol. 15, pp. 37-38.*

Forasmuch as the wearing of long haire after the manner of Ruffians and barbarous Indians, hath begun to invade new England contrary to the rule of Gods word wch sayth it is a shame for a man to wear long hair, as also the Commendable Custome generally of all the Godly of our nation until wthin this few yeares Wee the Magistrates who have subscribed this paper (for the clearing of our owne innocency in this behalfe) doe declare & manifest our dislike & detestation against the wearing of such long haire, as against a thing uncivil and unmanly whereby men doe deforme themselves, and offend sober & modest men, & doe corrupt good manners. Wee doe therefore earnestly entreat all the Elders of this Jurisdiction (as often as they shall see cause) to manifest their zeal against it, in their Publike administrations, and to take Care that the members of their respective Churches bee not defiled therewth, that so such as shall proove obstinate & will not reforme themselves may have god & man to bear witnes against them

The third Month. 10. day 1649

Thomas fflint
Rob: Bridges
Simon Bradstreet
Jo: Endicott Govr
Tho Dudley Dep Dep Govr
Rich Bellingham
Richard Saltonstall
Increase Nowell
William Hibbins

The fight against fashion continued in the General Court in 1651 (Records of the Governor and Company of the Massachusetts Bay in New England, *vol. 3, pp. 243-244), but with mixed success as the* Records and Files of the Quarterly Courts in Essex County Massachusetts *(Salem, 1911-21), vol. 1, pp. 274-276, show.*

1651: 4 OCTOBER.

Although severall declarations & orders have bin made by this Court agaynst excesse in apparrill, both of men & women, which hath not yet taken that efect which were to be desired, but on the contrary we cannot but to our greife take notice that intollerable excesse & bravery hath crept in uppon us, & especially amongst people of meane condition, to the dishonor of God, the scandall of or pfession, the consumption of estates, & altogether unsuteable to our povertie; & although we acknowledge it to be a matter of much difficultie, in regard of the blindnes of mens mindes & the stubbournnes of theire wills, to set downe exact rules to confine all sorts of psons, yet we cannot but accoumpt it our duty to comend unto all sorts of psons a so-ber & moderate use of those blessings which, beyond our expectation, the Lord hath been pleased to afford unto us in this wildernes, & also to declare or utter detestation & dislike that men or women of meane condition, educations, & callinges should take uppon them the garbe of gentlemen, by the wearinge of gold or silver lace, or buttons, or poynts at theire knees, to walke in greate bootes; or women of the same ranke to weare silke or tiffany hoodes or scarfes, which though allowable to persons of greater estates, or more liberall education, yet we cannot but judge it intollerable in psons of such like condition; its therefore ordred by this Court & the authoritie thereof, that no person within this jurisdiction, or any of theire relations depending uppon them, whose visible estates, reall & psonall, shall not exceede the true & indeferent value of two hundred poundes, shall weare any gold or silver lace, or gold or silver buttons, or any bone lace aboue two shillinge p yard, or silke hoodes or scarfes, uppon the penalty *of ten shillinges for every such offence; & every such delinquent to be psented by the graund jury. And forasmuch as distinct & perticuler rules in this case, suteable to the estate or qualitie of each pson, cannot easily be given, it is further ordred by the authoritie afforesd, that the select men of every towne, or the major part of them, are hereby enabled & required & *required*, from time to time, to have regard & take notice of apparrill in any of the inhabitants of theire severall townes respectively, & whosoever they shall judge to exceed theire rankes & abillitie in the costlynes or fashion of theire apparrill in any respect, especially in the wearinge of ribons & great bootes, (leather beinge a commodie scarce in this country,) the sd select men shall have power to assesse such persons so offendinge in any of the perticulers above mentioned, in the country rate, at 200li, accordinge to that proportion that such men use to pay to whom such apparrill is suteable & allowed; pvided, that this law shall not extend to the restraynt of any magistrate or other publicke officer of this jurisdiction, theire wives & children, who are left to theire discretion in wearinge of apparrill, or any settled millitary officer, or souldier in the time of military servise, or any other whose education &

imployment have beene above the ordinary degree, or whose estates have beene considerable, though now decayed; & this order to take place & be of force two moneths after the end of this session of Court.

Court held in Salem,   1652:
Jonas Fairbankes presented for wearing great boots. Discharged, it appearing that he did not wear them after the law was published.

Henry Bullocke fined for excess in his apparel in boots, ribbons, gold and silver lace, etc. Witnesses: The whole town, and in particular Lt. Lat[h]rup, Rich. Prince and Joh[n] Porter.

Marke Hoscall of Salem fined for excess in his apparel, wearing broad lace.

Court held in Salem, November 1652:
The wife of Austin Killum, presented for wearing a silk hood. Continued.

Wife of Thomas Fiske of Wenham fined for wearing a tiffany hood.

Alice, daughter of William Flint, presented for wearing a silk hood. He was proved to be worth over 200li., and she was discharged.

The civil courts were not the only opponents of fashion. The Rev. Ezekiel Rogers, the first minister of Rowley, Massachusetts, carried the fray into his own home. The following document was printed in the New-England Historical and Genealogical Register, *vol. 13 (1859), pp. 313-314.*

In the year 1665, five years after the death of the Rev. Ezekiel Rogers, his relative Ezekiel Rogers, son of the Rev. Nathaniel Rogers of Ipswich, brought an action against the widow of his uncle, which occasioned the following testimonies:

"The testimony of Maximilian Jewett saith that I heard our Mr. Rogers of Rowley expresse himselfe very much dissatisfied with the carriage of Ezekiel Rogers, in particular his familiarity with John Smith, his servant, the Scotchman, & that in some times going behind the meeting house, which bred fears & jealousies in his mind."

"Deposition of John Pickard—Ezekiel Rogers said the said

Ezekiel pleased him not, but said were it not for respect to my cousin deceased, I would give him nothing—he gave three reasons why he would give him no more (£ 160)—1. Because he refused to dwell with him. 2. Because he would not keep at the College though there he would have maintayned him. 3. Because he spoke to his mother to have his haire cutt but could not get it done.''

"Samuel Brocklebank testified that Ezekiel Rogers sayd he would give him no more, for he never promised him any thing, but upon condition that he would be guided by him and listen to his counsel.''

Testimony of Richard Swan—"The Rev. Ezekiel Rogers expressed trouble of mind about Ezekiel for he had sent for him to come to him & he came not, nor would he cutt off a locke of his hair at his desire.''

Mrs. Margaret Rogers, aged 55, widow of Rev. Nathaniel Rogers, testified about her son Ezekiel—"'Further at another time since the deponent went to the said Mr. Ezekiel Rogers to speake with him about her son Ezekiel's haire yt was complayned of to be too long, but when Mr. Ezekiel Rogers would have her son bound to let his haire be no longer than to yc lower tip of his eares, she told him she would never yield to such a snare for her child, tho' he never had penny of him while he lived.''

Mr. Rogers thus writes in his will—"I do also protest against all the evil fashions & guises of this age, both in apparel & that general disguisement of long ruffian-like haire, a custom most generally taken up at that time, when the grave and modest wearing of hair was a part of the reproach of Christ, as appears by the term of round-heads,& was carried on with a high hand, notwithstanding the known offence of so many godly persons, & without public expression of their reason for any such liberty.

*In 1672 another leading clergyman lent his voice to the attack on
long hair. John Eliot and his congregation's petition is printed in the*
Proceedings *of the Massachusetts Historical Society, second series,
vol. 29, pp. 98-99.*

The humble Petition of some of the people that lyve under the
Jurisdiction of the massachusets government, unto our honored
Magistrates this 5 day of march 1672

Sheweth

That whareas it hath pleased our ever honored Magistrates to send
their letters to the Chur[ch]es, to move us to a liberal contribution
towards the Colledg, and in one of those letters declared that if any
of the good people have any objecsion you give us leave to propose
it, and also are pleased to promise us, to doe your indeavor to
remove the same. We take the boldnesse to propose an objecsion, not
with any intent to shorten either our owne or others hands to so good
and pius a work, as we trust we shaall make it appeare by our actions, but our only scope is, to indevor the removal of an evyl (as it
appeareth to us) in the educasion of youth at the colledg, and that is,
that they are brought up in such pride as doth no wayes become such
as are brought up for the holy service of the lord, either in the
magistracy, or ministry especialy, and in perticular in their long
haire, which lust first took head, and brake out at the Colledg so far
as we understand and remember, and now it is got into our pulpets,
to the great greife and offence of many godly hearts in the Country
we find in the scriptures that the sons of the prophets, and such as
were dedicated to god, were brought up in a way of mortification and
humility. we beseech you to consider amos. 2. 11. 12. I raised up of
your sons to be prophets and of your young men to be nazarites, is it
not even thus o ye children of Israel saith the lord, but yc have given
the nazarits wine to drink. Consider also pro. 16. 31 the hoary head is
a crowne of glory if it be found in the way of righteousnesse, and are
those haires so found, that are defiled with this lust? we beseech you
consider, whether all other lusts which have so incorigibly brake in
upon our youth, have not first sprung from the incorrigablenesse of
this lust our humble request is that you would please to use all due in-
deavours to cure this evyl. and so we commend you to the lord and to

the word of his grace and remaine your Umble petecinors att the thron of grac to assist and inable you in all your waighty consarns and remain

your worships humble

petitioners

Thomas ffoster:	Giles paison
Abraham Neuall Seaner	John Parpoint
Isaac Neuell	Samuell Ruggles
Jacob nuell	Robbert williams
Robert Pepper	Samuell williams
abraham how	Edward Bridge
Samu'l may	edward paison
John watson	Ritchard goad
Ralph hemenway	John Eliot
	John Bowles
	Danil bwer: [Brewer]
	Samuel gary
	Robert Seauer
	John poley
	Edward morris

In 1675 a loose confederation of New England Indians under King Philip unleashed a furious war against the Puritans, who read this action as God's judgement against them for many "Provoking evills" they had committed. The following document from the Records of the Governor and Company of the Massachusetts Bay in New England *was the result. It is found in vol. 5, pp. 59-61.*

Whereas the most wise & holy God, for severall yeares past, hath not only warned us by his word, but chastized us wth his rods, inflicting upon us many generall (though lesser) judgments, but we have neither heard the word nor rod as wee ought, so as to be effectually humbled for our sinns to repent of them, reforme, and amend our wayes; hence it is the righteous God hath heightened our calamjty, and given comission to the barbarous heathen to rise up against us, and to become a smart rod and severe scourge to us, in burning & depopulating severall hopefull plantations, murdering many of our people of all sorts, and seeming as it were to cast us off, and putting us to shame, and not going forth wth our armies, heereby speaking aloud to us to search and try our wayes, and turne againe unto the Lord our God, from whom wee have departed with a great backsliding.

1. The Court, apphending there is too great a neglect of discipline in the churches, and especially respecting those that are their children, through the non acknowledgment of them according to the order of the gospell; in watching over them, as well as chattechising of them, inquireing into theire spirittuall estates, that, being brought to take hold of the covenant, they may acknouledge & be acknouledged according to theire relations to God & to his church, and theire obligations to be the Lords, and to approoue themselves so to be by a suiteable profession & conversation; and doe therefore solemnly recomend it unto the respective elders and brethren of the severall churches throughout this jurisdiction to take effectuall course for reformation herein.

*2. Whereas there is manifest pride openly appearing amongst us in that long haire, like weomens haire, is worne by some men, either their oune or others haire made into perewiggs, and by some weomen wearing borders of haire, and theire cutting, curling, & imodest laying out their haire, which practise doeth prevayle & increase, especially amongst the younger sort,—

This Court doeth declare against this ill custome as offencive to them, and divers sober christians amongst us, and therefore doe hereby exhort and advise all persons to use moderation in this respect; and further, doe impower all grand juries to present to the County Court such persons, whither male or female, whom they shall judge to exceede in the premisses; and the County Courts are hereby authorized to proceed against such delinquents either by admonition, fine, or correction, according to theire good discretion.

3. Notwthstanding the wholesome lawes already made by this Court for restreyning excesse in apparrell, yet through corruption in many, and neglect of due execution of those lawes, the evill of pride in apparrell, both for costlines in the poorer sort, & vaine, new, strainge fashions, both in poore & rich, wth naked breasts and armes, or, as it were, pinioned wth the addition of superstitious ribbons both on haire & apparrell; for redresse whereof, it is ordered by this Court, that the County Courts, from time to time, doe give strict charge to present all such persons as they shall judge to exceede in that kinde,

and if the grand jury shall neglect theire duty herein, the County Court shall impose a fine upon them at their discretion.

And it is further ordered, that the County Court, single magistrate, Comissioners Court in Boston, have heereby power to sumon all such persons so offending before them, and for the first offence to admonish them, and for each offence of that kinde afterwards to impose a fine of tenn shillings upon them, or, if unable to pay, to inflict such punishment as shall be by them thought most suiteable to the nature of the offence; and the same judges above named are heereby impowred to judge of and execute the lawes already extant against such excesse.

Whereas it may be found amongst us, that mens thresholds are sett up by Gods thresholds, and mans posts besides Gods posts, espeacially in the open meetings of Quakers, whose damnable heresies, abominable idolatrys, are hereby promoted, embraced, and practised, to the scandall *of religion, hazard of souls, and provocation of divine jealousie against this people, for prevention & reformation whereof, it is ordered by this Court and the authority thereof, that every person found at a Quakers meeting shall be apphended, ex officio, by the constable, and by warrant from a magistrate or comissioner shall be comitted to the house of correction, and there to have the discipline of the house applied to them, and to be kept to worke, wth bread & water, for three days, and then released, or else shall pay five pounds in money as a fine to the county for such offence; and all constables neglecting their duty in not faithfully executing this order shall incurr the penalty of four pounds, upon conviction, one third whereof to the informer.

And touching the law of importation of Quakers, that it may be more strictly executed, and none transgressing to escape punishment,—

It is heereby ordered, that the penalty to that law averred be in no case abated to lesse than twenty pounds.

5. Whereas there is so mutch profanes amongst us in persons turning their backs upon the publick worship before it be finished and the blessing pronounced,—

It is ordered by this Court, that the officers of the churches, or selectmen, shall take care to prevent such disorders, by appointing persons to shutt the meeting house doores, or any other meete way to attaine the end.

6. Whereas there is much disorder & rudenes in youth in many congregations in time of the worship of God, whereby sin & prophaness is greatly increased, for reformation whereof,—

It is ordered by this Court, that the select men doe appoint such place or places in the meeting house for children or youth to sit in where they may be most together and in publick view, and that the officers of the churches, or selectmen, doe appoint some grave & sober person or persons to take a particcular care of and inspection over them, who are heereby required to present a list of the names of such, who, by their oune observance or the information of others, shallbe found delinquent, to the next magistrate or Court, who are impowred for the first offence to admonish them, for the second offence to impose a fine of five shillings on theire parents or gouernnors, or order the children to be whipt, and if incorrigible, to be whipt wth ten stripes, or sent to the house of correction for three dayes.

*7. Whereas the name of God is prophaned by comon swearing and cursing in ordinary comunication, which is a sin that growes amongst us, and many heare such oathes and curses, and concealles the same from authority, for reformation whereof, it is ordered by this Court, that the lawes already in force against this sin be vigorously prosecuted; and, as addition thereunto, it is further ordered, that all such persons who shall at any time heare prophane oathes and curses spoken by any person or persons, and shall neglect to disclose the same to some magistrate, comissioner, or constable, such persons shall incurr the same penalty provided in that law against swearers.

8. Whereas the shamefull and scandelous sin of excessive drinking, tipling, & company keeping in tavernes, &c, ordinarys, grows upon us, for reformation whereof,—

It is comended to the care of the respective County Courts not to license any more publick houses then are absolutely necessary in any toune, and to take care that none be licenst but persons of approved sobriety and fidelity to law and good order; and that licensed houses be regulated in theire improovement for the refreshing & enteinment of travailers & strangers only, and all toune dwellers are heereby strictly enjoyned & required to forbeare spending their time or estates in such comon houses of enterteynment, to drincke & tiple, upon penalty of five shillings for every offence, or, if poore, to be whipt, at the discretion of the judge, not exceeding five stripes; and every ordinary keeper, permitting persons to transgress as aboue said, shall incurr the penalty of five shillings for each offence in that kinde; and any magistrate, comissioner, or selectmen are impowred & required vigorously to putt the abovesaid law in execution.

During the heat of the long hair controversy, the Rev. Michael Wigglesworth of Malden tried to shed a little light on its opponents for the students of Harvard, its primary advocates. His sermon has been published in the New England Historical and Genealogical Register, *vol. 1 (1847), pp. 368-371.*

We come now to speak of hair, and pride therein, but before we begin, remember these two general Rules formerly layd down. First that the Scriptures hath not set down every particular form and fashion of apparrel, but hath left us General Rules, from which we are to make application to this and that particular. It sets you down the general Rules to walk by, and those are sufficient to direct our conscience in ye practise of particulars. 2ly The Scriptures do not condemn every particular unlawful or unseemly Fashion in Apparrel, or manner of wearing the hair: but there are General rules given by which such are to be Censured. Theref: when we are reproved for such & such fashions, let no man say, I pray tel me what rule in Scripture condemn such apparrel or such length of hair. There be several rules, which you may be guilty of breaking.

In this point of long hair many things may be said. Some lay this down for a position, that it is not lawful to make an ornament of an excrement, and that it is absurd as wel as to affect long nayles, such as Nebuchadnezzar is said to have had. Dan. 4, 33. But this is certain, that a man is not to disfigure himself either in hair or apparrel.

Consider these following 5 Propositions.

1 Prop. That length of hair, which either the special appointmt of God, or nature allows, is not unlawfull. The Nazarite of old might let his hair grow, for by Gods special appointment no Rassur was to come upon his head. Numb. 6. 5.—So also that which nature allows is lawfull. That length of hair which either the ornament, of nature, or the necessity & comfort of nature alloweth, is lawfull. First for the ornament of nature. Hair is given a man to preserve him from the deformity of baldness, therefore so much hair as may preserve his head from baldness is for ye ornament of nature, and therefore

lawfull. 2ly That which the comfort of nature calls for wch may be for ye warmth of the head and of those parts which be contiguous to it, so much hair as may attain this end is not unlawfull. No man can justly condemn such a length of hair as is worn for this end and use, and as may attain this end, provided that the circumstances of place, person & season of ye year be also observed herein. For to weare thus much hair, when there is need off it for ye preservation & comfort of life can no more be condemned, then to wear an Artificiall covering.

Now then this followeth. If any shall under pretence of preserving the health and comfort of their heads & lives wear their hair over their necks or bands (or doublet collar) it is an unseemly thing, and hath not any foot hold that I know of in Gods word. Hence for young men and such as are of healthfull constitutions, whose heads can bear cold (and especially in warm weather when there is no need of it) for such to wear it at this length is justly offensive to the people of God. And if a man once go beyond those bounds of Gods speciall appointmet, & what nature alloweth or calls for, I know not where he will stay. If ye affect to go any whit beyond this I know not where ye will stop untill ye grow like the veriest Ruffian in ye world.

Be not offended with persons that are weak or in ye winter time find a need of it, if they wear it so as may be a help to them, as a little below their ears.

2 Proposit:

That length of hair which is womanish and savors of effeminacy, is unlawfull. The scpt gives you an express rule for this I Cor. 11 14. 15. It is against the nature of a man. Every length of hair that is a badge of it, when it tends to make man womanlike, or unmanlike, is unlawfull. Nature hath given to man the natural temper hotter than the woman, and therefore short hair is given to the man as a naturall sign of his rule. So that it is a sin against nature to affect or wear womanish hair, it is unseemly & against the light of nature, against naturall decency. And though diverse of ye Heathen did wear long hair, yet they did it rather out of a neglect of themselves, then for ornament; yea many of them accounted it their greatest ornament to wear short hair. Seneca in one of his Epistles stands and wonders why men should nourish their hair, for if they wear it for ornament saith hee, there are many horses have greater mains, then thou hast an head of hair. And many of them say, that there are few that wear long hair inclining to a womanish length but they are either soft and womanish spirits, or else filthy and full of vice. The womans hair is given her for a covering: Hence when men shall wear their hair so as may be for a covering, that is so as may be tyed up on the top of their head, or be turned back and tyed behind in their necks, it is a most effeminate thing. I Tim. 2. 9. It argues much wantonness when men shall affect a kind of bravery as now adayes they do by curling or frizeling of their hair, and parting it with a seam in ye middest, it argues much effeminacy. The Lord abhorrs such vanity in women, but for men to do it is a most loathsom thing, and a fashion altogether unbeseeming a christian.

3 Propos:

That length of hair which is an effect or a badge of pride and vanity, though in it self it be nothing, yet it is unlawfull for thee, although it might be lawfull for another man. Suppose it were lawfull to weare longer hair then is usuall, yet if it be a badge of pride in thy heart it is unlawful to thee; and if thy right eye cause thee to offend or thy right hand, pluck out the one, cut off thee other and cast it from thee. If it nourish pride in thy heart, away with it: else thou makest provision for the flesh and lusts thereof in keeping it to be a snare unto thee.

obj: oh but it is comfortable and needful.

Ans. I say that unnecessary length of hair which nourisheth pride in you, away with that.

obj: But such a good man wears his hair as long, and why may not I?

Ans. That which is one mans meat may be another mans poison. It may be he wears it so out of a neglect of himself, whereas it would nourish pride in thy heart. Or he may have a need of it or some other reason for it, which thou hast not.

4 Proposition.

That length of Hair which exceeds the ordinary length worn by persons that are most godly and gracious in ye country where you live, & ye Relation wherein you stand, that length is unlawful, you are bound to imitate the generality of the best: unless this Age of good men be degenerated from former examples without cause. I know examples are not to be any mans rule, but the word is to be my Rule and the word gives me this Rule, what soever things are honest, what soever things are lovely & of good report &c. think of these things Phil 4. 8; 9 what soever you have learned & received, heard and seen in me, do v 9: So that though no mans example be my rule, yet in ye Application of my conscience to ye Rule I look to ye examples of the best & most grave and sober yt we live amongst. And why should any one affect the fashion of a Ruffian, before the fashion of a godly grave person? or why the examples of degenerate later times be followed rather then the better examples of former times? what the Apostle speaks of Apparrel I Pet. 3: 3. 4. 5. may be applyd to this of hair. And in the I Cor. 11 16. If any man seem to be contentious we have no such custom with the churches of God. It hath been a loathsom thing to all ye Godly in former ages to wear long hair. It hath not been their manner amongst civil nations to wear long hair. It was a dishonour in former times for a man that had any love to Religion to wear a lock.

5 Prop. That length of hair which is offensive unto the weak is unlawfull. obj: But they take offense where there is none given. Ans. There may be weakness in taking offense, yet in some cases we ought not to offend the weak, though it be their weakness to be offended. Rom. 14, 15. 20. we must not offend our Brother with our meat. I Cor. 8: last. I will eat no flesh for ever rather then offend my Brother. Q. when ought we to tender our Brothers weakness and to avoyd that which grieves him, & when ought we not to regard it?

Ans. If it be a duty for you to do this or that, then if others be offended at it, it is no matter. Wo to the world becaus of offenses. In this case you must not forbear a duty becaus others wil be offended. Christ himself was an offence to many in this case.

But 2ly If it may be as wel forborn as done, then I am not to be an offence to others in an indifferet thing. As ye Apostle I: Corinth: 8. ult. I wil rather never eat flesh then offend my Brother (that is some kind of flesh that the Jews scrupled) for in offending my Brother thus I should sin, & offend God. So for your hair; It may be in winter time you may need it longer to keep you warm, but in sumer you need it not, therefore it is then a sin to offend others in wearing it. 3ly If a Brother be offended and he gives his reason, though it be a weak reason, yet I am to abstain from that which may offend him, so as it be indifferent. 4ly when the case is so, that there is no other offended if I forbear such a fashion or such length of hair, & many are offended that I use it; I ought in this case to forbear it. Or if in some things offence will be taken on both sides by some, a man is at his liberty: but yet be sure to chuse that which shall give least offence. Now I do not think that ye consciences of any wil be offended at your short hair, unless you should shamefully disfigure your selves, wch were a vanity & sin to do.

Thus you have had the Rules that God giveth us about the wearing of hair and apparrel: and for excess in these things the wrath of God is so great, that he brings ye sword upon a land to destroy it, as you see in the text. It is such an uncurable evil, that men and women wil never leave it, til the Lord take it away by force and violence. Consider then, can you wear long hair without offence to some, or without pride and vanity in your own heart. 2ly If you could wear it wth out offence or pride, why wil you do it in this country, where most of ye people of God wear short hair. No man thinks you the better for ye long hair. For us to follow fashions and to wear long hair, it doth not become us, & the humility and meanness of that condition that God sets us in; especially for scholars and such as should be most exemplary.

3ly Why should we wear it at such a time as this when every one useth it, the very basest sort of persons, every Ruffian, every wild-Irish, every hang-man, every varlet and vagabond shall affect long hair, shall men of place and honour esteem it an honour unto them?

4ly Why wil you come so near to the brink of an evil. He that sathan can perswade to wear his hair an inch too long, he wil be brought to wear it much longer. Take 3 considerations with you.

1. God calls every christian to walk not onely sincerely but exactly. Is this exactness to go neer the brink of ye pit? 2ly walk safely. If there be a sin in long hair it is certain it is no sin to wear short hair; chuse that which is most safe. 3ly Consid. what an evil it wil be when God awakens thy consciece. You may wallow in all sins now, but the least sin when God casts it into ye eye of consciece wil trouble you.

VI. HEAVEN AND EARTH

Religion was the touchstone of all New England life. Why did religion permeate Puritan culture so deeply at every point? Did Man's nature require religion? Why? How could Man gain salvation? Could he earn salvation by his own efforts? What aid did he have in the search for salvation? What were the chief strengths and weaknesses of the Puritan worship service? What can you tell about them from the complaints of the ministers themselves about their congregations? Why was heresy so serious a crime? Who was most susceptible to heretical teaching? What did the Puritans urge as the best antidote to heresy? Why? What were its strengths? Who benefitted from early catechizing besides the children? In what ways? Who was responsible for the religious instruction of New English children? Were they successful in their own lights? What do the self-criticisms of the Puritan "jeremiad" (named for the lamentations of the Biblical Jeremiah) reveal about New England culture? Are they accurate descriptions of social reality? Why?

The religious life of the Puritans, as in most societies, began at an early age. The following advice of Cotton Mather (1663-1728) was typical of the Puritan emphasis on beginning religious instruction "betimes". It is taken from the preface of The Man of God Furnished *(Boston, 1708) which Paul Leicester Ford reprinted on pp. 263-269 of his edition of* The New England Primer *(New York, 1897). Following Mather's advice are selections from the Westminster Assembly Catechism of 1649, the joint product of 156 Puritan divines and laymen called by the Roundhead Parliament in 1643. Its 107 questions, requiring answers from eight to one hundred words in length, was considered "Shorter" than the normal run of catechisms*

in use at that time. In New England it was widely printed beside The
New England Primer *until well into the 19th century, and thus
served as the religious introduction to New England life for the great
majority of its children.*

An ADDRESS to, *(them that should be) The* INSTRUCTORS *of
the Ignorant:*

That the Principles of the *Christian Religon* should be *Betimes*
instilled into those, who are under our influences, there is all the
Reason imaginable; there are none but what confess it infinitely
Reasonable. That the way of instilling the *Christian Religion,* by
Catechising, or a conference carried on with *Question* and *Answer,* is
very Necessary, and highly agreeable to awaken the *Attention,* and
Enlighten the *Understanding* of the *Catechumens*; this also is the
confession of all, who have considered, but how *Mankind* is to be
dealt withal.

The very many Sorts of *Catechisms,* which have been Published
(the Catalogue whereof would arise to some *Hundreds*), and the huge
Numbers of all Sorts (whereof some have arisen to very many *Hun-
dreds of Thousands*) have practically Expressed the sense of the
Christian World: concerning the *Needfulness* and *Usefulness* of
Catechising.

All that have Read the *History* of the *Se*paration of the
Faithful, from the *Romish Babylon,* have been somewhat informed
of the mighty Consequence, whereof *Catechising* has been unto the
Reformation. Celebrated is the History of the Unsuccessful Attempts
which the *Popist Missionaries* made upon the *Vaudois*; the *Children*
were so well *Catechised,* it seems, the Seducers could have no Suc-
cess upon them. And the Church of *Rome* has taken the Alarum; the
Romanists also are become in their way indefatigable *Catechisers.*
The *Jesuites* especially, because they count themselves the greatest
Catechisers, boast themselves the greatest *Conservators* of *their
Christianity.* Yea, there is now scarce any *Sect,* of them who never
cease to *Pervert the Right wayes of the Lord,* but they are now got in-
to *this Way;* even those who decry all *Forms,* yet cannot keep out of
This: 'tis by *Incessant Catechising,* that they propose to attain their
Ends.

And, first, if it be the concern of any under Heaven, it cannot but
be *Yours,* O PARENTS, to *Catechise* your *Children,* in the *Princi-*

ples of the Doctrine of Christ. It is to YOU, first, that the Counsil of *Wisdom* is directed; Prov. 22 4. *Train up,* (or Catechize) *a Child, in the way he should go:* 'Tis to be done, even (as 'tis by some rend'red,) *In the very Entrance of his way.* The Things of God, and His Religion, are those whereof You have received this *Commandment* from Heaven; Deut. 6 7. *These things, Thou shalt teach them diligently unto thy Children, and thou shalt talk of them when thou sittest in thine House.* Without *Catechising* your *Children,* you never can yield Obedience to the *Holy Commandment:* Eph. 6. 4. *Bring up your Children, in the Nurture and Admonition of the Lord.* You see the *Word of a King:* we call upon you in the Name of that *Great King whose Name is Dreadful:* Let there be such *Power* in it, as to Awe you to do the Things that please Him.

Indeed You do very notably *Serve* yourselves, when you *Teach* your *Children.* Your *Well Catechised Children,* will be your *Comfort,* your *Honour. Happy the Man that has his Quiver full of them!* It may be, God will make them Sweet *Blessings* to you, if you *Teach* them to be true *Servants* to Him. Your *Children* will certainly be the more *Tractable,* the more *Orderly;* you will keep up *Your Authority* over them the better, for *your Catechising* of them.

If God Smile on your Serious Endeavours, with what *Joy* will you *See your Children walking in the Truth!* You will *Rejoyce greatly.* Your *Neighbourhood* will also have the Joyful Advantage of it. All the Neighbours that have any *Good* in them, or Love to *Good,* will Bless God, and Bless You, for the *Good,* which *Your well-instructed Children* do in the World. And *Religion* will thus, by your means, be Propagated unto the *Next Generation.* The *Law of Israel,* being thus *Made known to your Children,* the *Generation to come,* will reap the *Harvest* of your Excellent Endeavours; Yea, the *Children that are to be Born, will arise, and declare it unto their Children;* and they will *Set their Hope in God, & keep His Commandments.* Or, should the Children miscarry [which God forbid!] after you have Endeavoured their best Education in *Catechising* of them, You will still have this Peace of Conscience, *I did my Duty!* But if the *Duty* which you owe unto the *Children,* that are committed unto you by God, be left Undone, it must needs leave such a *Sting* upon the Conscience, as upon the *Death* of these Poor *Children,* or your own, will be a thousand times *more Bitter than Death.* By *Cathechizing* your *Children* you Enrich their Minds, with incomparable *Treasures:* You lay a *Foundation* to render them *Temples* of God, wherewith no Artificial Structures, tho' never so stately, are to be compared. But if they are kept *Ignorant* of the *Things of their Peace*, this *Ignorance* will be, but the *Mother of Destruction* unto them. You know the word of God: Prov. 19, 2. *That the Soul be without Knowledge it is not Good.* Your *Children will never be full of Goodness*, if they be not *fill'd with Knowledge.* If the *Image of God* be *Renewed* upon them, the first Lineaments of it, will be *in Knowledge*. Without *That*, they will Retain the *Image* of *Satan* on them; they will Stumble along in the dark *Empire* of *Satan*, the *Ruler of the Darkness of this World;* they will be a *Morsel* for *Satan* at the last: *Brought forth for the Murderer!*

The *Souls* of your *Children* make a Cry in your Ears, O *Parents;* a cry enough to break an Heart of Adamant. They are *Born Children of Wrath;* and when they grow up, you have no way to *Save* them from the dreadful *Wrath* of God, if you do not *Catechisé* them in the *Way of Salvation.* They cry to you; *O our dear Parents; Acquaint us with the Great God, and His Glorious Christ that so Good may come unto us! Let us not go from your Tender Knees, down to the Place of Dragons.* Oh! Not *Parents*, but *Ostriches:* Not *Parents* but *Prodigies!* What, but more cruel than the *Sea-Monsters* are the *Parents*, who will not be moved by such Thoughts as these, to *Draw out* the *Breasts* of the *Catechism*, unto their *Young Ones!* One would think, *Parents*, Your own *Bowels*, if you have not *Monstrously* lost them, would Suggest enough to perswade you unto the *Pleasant Labours* of the *Catechism.*

You cannot be *Children of God* your selves, if you are not Sollicitous, that your *Children* should become the *Servants of God:* If you can bear to see them *Traitors* to *God*, and *Vassals* of the *Devil.* It is the Chracter of every Pious Parent in the World; Gen. 18.19. *I Know him, that he will command his Children, and Household after him, and they shall keep the way of the Lord.*

Both of the *Parents* are under Obligations to this *Work of God.* Even the *MOTHERS* must not reckon themselves Excused; no, but as in some regard, their *Opportunities* to *Catechise* the *Children* are Singular, so are their *Obligations.* It was well for *Solomon*, that he had his Mother *Bathsheba;* It was well for *Timothy*, that he had his Mother *Eunice*, to *Catechise* him. Oh ye Handmaids of the Lord; The *Law of Christ*, should be so Set home upon your *Children*, that it may be said unto them, *Forsake not the Law of thy Mother!* Your *Children* may say, *In Sin did my Mother conceive me.* Why should they not also have cause to say, *My Mother did what she could, that I might be Saved out of my Sin; and come to the Knowledge of my Saviour!* You have the *Children* very much with you; You *Feed* them; you *Dress* them; They fly to your *Wing;* you may *Catechise* them every day; you may be continually dropping something of the *Catechism* upon them: Some *Honey out of the Rock!*

And the *Masters* must also be Put in mind, that the *Servants* in the Family are their *Children*. The *Servants* also must be *Catechised;* give them some *Liesure* to Learn the *Catechism;* Some *Reward*, when they have duely Learnt it. Let them on this Account have cause Eternally to acknowledge the Compassion of God unto them, in bringing them to Live in a *Family*, where such care was taken of them.

We bespeak, *All Hands to the Work*. It must be the Work of the SCHOOL too. The *School-master*, the *School-mistress*, must be a *Catechist*. In some Reformed Places, the Magistrate countenances none to keep a *School*, but what appears with a *Testimonial*, of their *Ability*, and their *Disposition* particularly, [*Aptitudinis ad munus illud, imprimis Puerorum Catechizationem*] for the Work of *Religious Catechising*. We read, *The Little ones have their Angels*. To keep a *School*, is a most heavy, grievous, Wearisome Work; It is hardly ever sufficiently Recompenced. But then, to *Catechise* the Children, and bring them to *Know the Holy Scriptures*, this is a Noble Work; we had almost call'd it *A Work for Angels*. Be not *Weary* of this *Welldoing*. Certainly, Tis a Nobler Work, to make the Little Ones know their *Saviour*, than to know their *Letters*. The Lessons of *Jesus* are Nobler things than the Lessons of *Cato*. A Sanctifying *Transformation* of their Souls, were a Nobler Thing, than meerly to construe *Ovids Metamorphosis*. Every Week, Let the *School* have one or two *Catechetical Exercises*. And when you set your *Scholars*, to Write *Copies*, or make *Latin*, why may not the *Catechism* afford *Materials* for them? This would make the *Golden Nails* to stick the Faster in their Minds. By such *Methods* you may be so Serviceable to them in their Highest Interests, as to make a Real Problem of that which in the *Schools* they sometimes *Thematize* upon; *Whether Children may not be as much Endebted unto their* TUTORS, *as unto their Parents?*

But it is a point of Extreme Importance in a *Catechising*, that the *Understandings* of the *Children*, should have the Truths of the Gospel in them, as well as their *Memories*.

The SHORTER CATECHISM

Agreed upon by the Reverend

Assembly of Divines *at Westminster*

Quest *What is the chief End of Man?*

Answ. Man's chief End is to Glorify God, and to Enjoy Him for ever.

Q. *What Rule hath God given to direct us how we may glorify and enjoy Him?*

A. The Word of God which is contained in the Scriptures of the Old and New Testament, is th only Rule to direct us how we may glorify and enjoy him.

Q. *What do the Scriptures principally teach?*

A. The Scriptures principally teach, what Man is to believe concerning God, and what duty God requireth of Man.

Q. *What is God?*

A. God is a Spirit, Infinite, Eternal, and Unchangeable, in His Being, Wisdom, Power, Holiness, Justice, Goodness and Truth.

Q. *Are there more Gods than One?*

A. There is but ONE only, the living and true God.

Q. *How many Persons are there in the God-head?*

A. There are Three Persons in the God-Head, the Father, the Son, and the Holy Ghost, & these Three are One GOD the same in Substance, equal in Power & Glory.

Q. *What are Gods Works of Providence?*

A. God's Works of Providence are his most holy, wise & powerful preserving & govering all his Creatures and all their Actions.

Q. *What Special Act of Providence did God exercise towards Man in the Estate wherein he was created?*

A. When God had created Man, He entred into a Covenant of Life with him, upon condition of perfect Obedience, forbidding him to Eat of the Tree of knowledge of good and evil upon pain of Death.

Q. *Did our first Parents continue in the estate wherein they were created?*

A. Our first Parents being left to the freedom of their own Will, fell from the estate wherein they were created, by sinning against God.

Q. *What is Sin!*

A. Sin is any want of Conformity unto, or Transgression of the Law of God.

Q. What was the Sin whereby our first Parents fell from the estate wherein they were created?

A. The Sin whereby our first Parents fell from the estate wherein they were created, was their eating the forbidden fruit.

Q. Did all Mankind fall in Adam's *first transgression?*

A. The Covenant being made with *Adam*, not only for himself but for his Posterity, all Mankind descending from him by ordinary Generation, sinned in him, & fell with him in his first transgression.

Q. Into what estate did the Fall bring Mankind?

A. The Fall brought Mankind into an estate of Sin and Misery.

Q. Wherein consists the sinfulness of that estate whereinto Man fell?

A. The sinfulness of that estate whereinto Man fell, consists in the Guilt of *Adam's* first Sin, the want of Original Righteousness, and the Corruption of his whole Nature, which is commonly called Original Sin, together withall actual Transgressions which proceed from it.

Q. What is the Misery of that estate whereinto Man fell?

A. All Mankind by their fall, lost Communion with God, are under his Wrath & Curse, and so made liable to all Miseries in this Life, to Death it self, and to the pains of Hell for ever.

Q. Did God leave all Mankind to perish in the estate of Sin & Misery?

A. God having out of his meer good pleasure from all Eternity, Elected some to everlasting Life, did enter into a Covenant of Grace, to deliver them out of the state of Sin & Misery, and to being them into a state of Salvation by a Redeemer,

Q. Who is the Redeemer of Gods Elect?

A. The only Redeemer of Gods Elect, is the Lord Jesus Christ, who being the eternal Son of God, became Man, and so was, and continues to be God and Man in two distinct Natures, and one Person for ever.

Q. How are we made Partakers of the Redemption purchased by Christ?

A. We are made Partakers of the Redemption purchased by Christ, by the effectual Application of it to us by his Holy Spirit.

Q. How doth the Spirit apply to us the Redemption purchased by Christ?

A. The Spirit applieth to us the Redemption purchased by Christ, by working Faith in us, & thereby uniting us to Christ in our effectual Calling.

Q. *What is effectual Calling?*

A. Effectual Calling is the Work of God's Spirit, whereby convincing us of our Sin & Misery, enlightning our Minds in the Knowledge of Christ, & renewing our Wills he doth perswade & enable us to embrace Jesus Christ, freely offered to us in the Gospel.

Q. *What Benefits do they that are effectually called partake of in this Life?*

A. They that are Effectually called, do in this Life partake of Justification, Adoption, Sanctification, & the several Benefits which in this Life do either accompany or flow from them.

Q. *What is Justification?*

A. Justification is an act of God's free Grace, wherein he pardoneth all our Sins, and accepteth us as righteous in his fight, only for the righteousness of Christ imputed to us, and received by Faith alone.

Q. *What is Adoption?*

A. Adoption is an Act of God's Free Grace, whereby we are received into the Number, and have Right to all the Priviledges of the Sons of God.

Q. *What is Sanctification?*

A. Sanctification is the Work of God's free Grace, whereby we are renewed in the whole Man, after the Image of God, & are enabled more & more to die unto Sin, & live unto Righteousness.

Q. *What are the Benefits which in this life do accompany or flow from Justification, Adoption, & Santification?*

A. The Benefits which in this Life do accompany or flow from Justification, Adoption or Sanctification, are assurance of God's love, peace of Conscience, joy in the Holy Ghost, increase of Grace, & perseverance therein to the end.

Q. *What benefits do Believers receive from Christ at their Death?*

A. The Souls of Believers are at their Death made perfect in

Holiness, & do immediately pass into Glory, & their Bodies being still united to Christ, do rest in their Graves till the Resurrection.

Q. *What benefits do Believers receive from Christ at the Resurrection?*

A. At the Resurrection Believers being raised up to Glory, shall be openly acknowledged & acquitted in the Day of Judgment, & made perfectly blessed in full enjoying of God, to all Eternity.

Q. *What is the Duty which God requires of Man?*

A. The Duty which God requires of Man, is Obedience to his revealed will.

Q. *What did God at first reveal to Man for the Rule of his Obedience?*

A. The Rule which God at first revealed to Man for his Obedience was the Moral Law.

Q. *Where is the Moral Law summarily comprehended?*

A. The Moral Law is summarily comprehended in the Ten Commandments.

Q. *What is the Sum of the Ten Commandments?*

A. The Sum of the Ten Commandments is, To love the Lord our God with all our Heart, with all our Souls, and with all our Strength, and with all our Mind, and our Neighbour as ourselves.

Q. *Is any Man able perfectly to keep the Commandments of God?*

A. No meer man since the Fall is able in this Life perfectly to keep the Commandments of God, but daily doth break them in Thought, Word and Deed.

Q. *Are all Transgressions of the Law equally heinous?*

A. Some Sins in themselves, & by reason of several Aggravations are more heinous in the fight of God than others.

Q. *What doth every sin deserve?*

A. Every Sin deserveth God's Wrath and Curse, both in this Life, and that which is to come.

Q. *What doth God require of us, that we may escape his Wrath and Curse, due unto us for Sin?*

A. To escape the Wrath & Curse of God due to us for Sin, God requireth of us Faith in Jesus Christ, Repentance unto Life, with the diligent use of alloutward Means whereby Christ communicateth to us the benefits of Redemption.

Q. *What is Faith in Jesus Christ?*

A. Faith in Jesus Christ is a saving Grace, whereby we receive and rest upon him alone for Salvation, as He is offered to us in the Gospel.

Q. *What is Repentance unto Life?*

A. Repentance unto Life, is a saving Grace, whereby a Sinner out of a true sense of his Sin, and apprehension of the Mercy of God in Christ, doth with grief & hatred of his Sin, turn from it unto God, with full purpose of, & endeavour after new Obedience.

Q. *What are the outward* & ordinary means whereby Christ com-*muniontelb to us the benefits of Redemption?*

A the outward and ordinary means whereby Christ communicateth to us the benefits of Redemption are his Ordinances, especially the Word, Sacraments & Prayer; all which are made effectual to the Elect for Salvation.

Q. *How is the word made effectual to Salvation?*

A. The Spirit of God maketh the Reading, but especially the Preaching of the Word an effectual Means of Convincing & Converting Sinners, and of building them up in Holiness & Comfort, through Faith unto Salvation.

Q. *How is the Word to be Read and Heard that it may become effectual to Salvation?*

A. That the Word may become effectual to Salvation, we must attend thereunto with diligence, Preparation & Prayer, receive it with Faith & Love, lay it up in our Hearts, & practice it in our Lives.

Q. *How doth the Sacraments become effectual means of Salvation?*

A. The Sacraments become effectual Means of Salvation, not from any vertue in them, or in him that doth administer them, but only by the blessing of Christ, and the working of the Spirit in them that by Faith receive them.

Q. *What is a Sacrament?*

A. A Sacrament is an holy Ordinance instituted by Christ, wherein by sensible Signs, Christ and the benefits of the New Covenant are represented, sealed, and applied to Believers.

Q. *Which are the Sacraments of the New Testament?*

A. The Sacraments of the New Testament, are Baptism, and the Lord's Supper.

*As soon as the young New English child was old enough to sit still,
it was taken to "meeting" (as Sunday worship service was called).
There the bare words of the catechism took on meaning and form.
Thomas Lechford, a visiting lawyer who adhered to the Church of
England, described a typical New England meeting in 1642 for the
readers of his* Plain Dealing or News from New England *(reprinted in
the* Collections *of the Massachusetts Historical Society, third series,
vol. 3 (1833), pp. 76-79.)*

The public worship is in as fair a meeting house as they can provide, wherein in most places they have been at great charges. Every
Sabbath or Lord's day they come together at Boston, by ringing of a
bell, about nine of the clock or before. The pastor begins with solemn
prayer continuing about a quarter of an hour. The teacher then
readeth and expoundeth a chapter, then a psalm is sung, whichever
one of the ruling elders dictates. After that the pastor preacheth a
sermon, and sometimes *ex tempore* exhorts. Then the teacher con-
cludes with prayer and a blessing.

Once a month is a sacrament of the Lord's Supper, whereof notice
is given usually a fortnight before, and then all others departing save
the church—which is a great deal less in number than those that go
away—they receive the sacrament, the ministers and ruling elders
sitting at the table, the rest in their seats, or upon forms. All cannot
see the minister consecrating unless they stand up and make a nar-
row shift. The one of the teaching elders prays before and blesseth
and consecrates the bread and wine, according to the words of
institution; the other prays after the receiving of all the members; and
next communion they change turns, he that began at that ends at this.
And the ministers deliver the bread in a charger to some of the chief,
and peradventure gives to a few the bread into their hands, and they
deliver the charger from one to another till all have eaten; in like
manner the cup, till all have drank, goes from one to another. Then a
psalm is sung, and with a short blessing the congregation is
dismissed. Anyone, though not of the church, may in Boston come in
and see the sacrament administered if he will. [*Marginal note:* Once
I stood without one of the doors, and looked in, and saw the administration. Besides I have had credible relation of all the particulars
from some of the members.] But none of any church in the country
may receive the sacrament there without leave of the congregation,
for which purpose he comes to one of the ruling elders who pro-

pounds his name to the congregation before they go to the sacrament.

About two in the afternoon they repair to the meeting house again, and then the pastor begins—as before noon—and a psalm being sung, the teacher makes a sermon. He was wont, when I came first, to read and expound a chapter also before his sermon in the afternoon. After and before his sermon, he prayeth.

After that ensues baptism, if there be any, which is done by either pastor or teacher in the deacon's seat, the most eminent place in the church, next under the elder's seat. The pastor most commonly makes a speech or exhortation to the church and parents concerning baptism, and then prayeth before and after. It is done by washing or sprinkling. One of the parents being of the church, the child may be baptized, and the baptism is into the name of the Father, and of the Son, and of the Holy Ghost. No sureties are required.

Which ended, follows the contribution, one of the deacons saying "Brethren of the congregation, now there is time left for contribution, wherefore as God hath prospered you, so freely offer." Upon some extraordinary occasions as building and repairing of churches or meeting houses, or other necessities, the ministers press a liberal contribution with effectual exhortations out of scripture. The magistrates and chief gentlemen first, and then the elders, and all the congregation of men, and most of them that are not of the church, all single persons, widows, and women in absence of their husbands, come up one after another one way, and bring their offerings to the deacon at his seat, and put it into a box of wood for the purpose, if it be money or papers; if it be any other chattel, they set it or lay it down before the deacons, and so pass another way to their seats again. This contribution is of money, or papers promising so much money (I have seen a fair gilt cup with a cover, offered there by one, which is still used at the communion), which monies and goods the deacons dispose towards the maintenance of the ministers and the poor of the church and the church's occasions, without making account, ordinarily.

But in Salem church, those only that are of the church offer in public; the rest are required to give to the ministry by collection at their houses. At some other places they make a rate upon every man as well within as not of the church, residing with them, towards the church's occasions; and others are beholding now and then to the General Court to study ways to enforce the maintenance of the ministry.

This done then follows the admission of members, or hearing matters of offense, or other things, sometimes till it be very late. If they have time, after this is sung a psalm, and then the pastor concludeth with a prayer and a blessing.

Upon the week days there are lectures in divers towns, and in Boston upon Thursdays, when Master Cotton teacheth out of the *Revelation*. There are days of fasting, thanksgiving, and prayers upon occasions,[1] but no holy days[2] except the Sunday.

In some churches nothing is read[3] on the first day of the week, or Lord's day, but a psalm dictated before or after the sermon, as at Hingham; there is no catechizing of children or others in any church (except in Concord church and in other places, of those admitted, in their receiving), the reason given by some is because when people come to be admitted, the church hath trial of their knowledge, faith, and repentance, and they want a direct scripture for ministers' catechizing, as if, "Go teach all nations, and train up a child in the

1. And why not set fasting days and times, and set feasts, as well as set Synods in the Reformed Churches?
2. And why not holy days as well as the fifth of November, and the days of Purim among the Jews? Besides, the commemoration of the blessed and heavenly mysteries of our ever blessed Saviour, and the good examples and piety of the saints? What time is there for the moderate recreation of youth and servants but after divine services on most of those days, seeing that upon the Sunday it is justly held unlawful? And sure enough, at New England, the masters will and must hold their servants to their labor more than in other countries well planted is needful. Therefore I think even they should do well to admit of some holy days too, as not a few of the wiser sort among them hold necessary and expedient.
3. Whereas in England every Sunday are read in public chapters and psalms in every church, besides the eleven or twelve commandments, epistle and gospel, the Creed and other good forms and catechizings, and besides what is read upon holy days and other days both in the parish and Cathedral and collegiate churches and in the universities and other chapels, the benefit whereof, doubtless, as wise men will acknowledge to be exceeding great, as well as public preaching and expounding.

way he should go,'' did not reach to ministers' catechizings. But, God be thanked, the General Court was so wise in June last as to enjoin or take some course for such catechizing, as I am imformed, but know not the way laid down in particular how it should be done.

Not everyone was welcome in the Bible Commonwealth or its meetinghouses, as the Massachusetts laws made clear in no uncertain terms. The following sections of the 1672 codification are found in W.H. Whitmore's edition of The Colonial Laws of Massachusetts *(Boston, 1889), pp. 154-156, 158.*

HERESIE, ERROR

Although no humane Power, be Lord over the Faith & *Consciences of men, yet because such as bring in damnable Heresies, tending to the subversion of the Christian Faith* & *distructions of the soules of men, ought duely to be restrained, from such notorious impieties.* It is therefore Ordered and declared by the Court. That if any *Christian* within this Jurisdiction, shall go about to subvert and destroy the *Christian Faith and Religion*, by broaching and maintaining any *Damnable Heresies*: as denying the immortality of the soule, or resurrection of the body, or any sin to be repented of in the regenerate, or any evil done by the outward man to be accounted sin, or denying that Christ gave himselfe a ransom for our sins, or shall affirm that we are not justifyed by his death and righteousnes, but by the perfections of our own works, or shall deny the morallity of the Fourth Commandement, or shall openly Condemn or oppose the Baptizing of Infants, or shall purposely depart the Congregation at the administration of that Ordinance, or shall deny the ordinance of Magistracy, or their Lawfull Authority to make war, or to punish the outward breaches of the first Table [of the Ten Commandments], or shall endeavour to seduce others to any of the errors or heresies above mentioned, every such person continuing obstinate therin, after due meanes of Conviction, shall be sentenced to Banishment. [1646, 44] . . .

9. Whereas there is a pernicious Sect commonly called Quakers lately arisen, who by word and writing, have published and maintained many dangerous and horrid tenents, and do take upon them to change & alter, the received laudable customes of our nation in giving *Civil respect to equals, or reverence to Superiors, whose notions tend to undermine the Authority of Civil Government, as also to destroy the Order of the churches, by denying all established formes of worship, and by withdrawing from the orderly church assemblies, allowed* & approoved, by all Orthodox professors of the trueth; and *instead thereof* & opposition thereunto, frequenting private meetings *of their own, Insinuating themselves into the minds of the Simpler, or such as are less affected to the Order* & Government of the Church *and Commonwealth, whereby divers of our Inhabitants have been infected and seduced, notwithstanding all former Lawes made, (upon experience of their arrogant bold obtrusions, to disseminate their principles amongst us) prohibiting their Comming into this Jurisdiction, they have not been deterred from their impetuous attempts, to undermine our peace, and hasten our ruine.* For prevention thereof this Court doth Order and Enact, That every person or persons of the Cursed sect of the Quakers, who is not an Inhabitant of, but found within this Jurisdiction, shall be apprehended (without warrant where no Magistrate is at hand) by any Constable, Commissioner or Select Man, and conveyed from Constable to Constable untill they come before the next Magistrate who shall Committ the sayd person or persons to Close Prison, there to remaine without Baile, untill the next Court of Assistants where they shall have a Legall tryall, by a speciall jury, and being Convicted to be of the sect of the *Quakers*, shall be sentenced to banishment upon paine of Death. . . .

4. . . .And if any person or persons within this Jurisdiction, shall henceforth entertain & conceale any such *Quaker* or *Quakers* or other *Blasphemous hereticks* (knowing them to be such) every such person shall forfeit to the Countrey, *Fourty shillings* for every houres entertainment and concealment of any *Quaker* or *Quakers*, &c. as aforesayd, and shall be Committed to prison as aforesayd, till the fines be fully satisfyed and payd.

5. And every person or persons that shall *incourage or defend* any of their pernicious wayes by speaking, writing, or meeting on the Lords day, or at any other time, shall after due meanes of conviction, incurr the penalty ensuing, *viz.* every person so meeting, shall pay to the use of the Country, for every time ten shillings & every one speaking in such meeting, shall forfeit five pounds.

6. If any person shall knowingly import into any harbour of this Jurisdiction, any *Quakers Books* or *Writings*, concerning their damnable opinions, he shall forfeit for every such book or writing *Five Pounds*, and whosoever shall disperse or conceale any such book or writing, and it be found with him or her, or in his or her house, &

143

shall not immediately deliver the same to the next N.
forfeit and pay *Five Pounds*, for dispersing or Conceah
Book or writing.

7. And every person or persons whatsoever, that sha revile the
office or person of Magistrates or Ministers, as is usuall with the
Quakers, such Person or Persons shall be *Severely Whipt*, or pay the
Summ of *Five Pounds*.

8. And every person that shall publish and maintaine, any
Heterodox or erroneous Doctrine, shall be liable to be questioned
and Censured by the County Court where he liveth, according to the
merit of his offence.

*The Puritans tried their utmost to keep their lives as well as the
Sabbath holy, but like all perfectionists their reach exceeded their
grasp. The 1658 regulations concerning the Sabbath come from* The
Colonial Laws of Massachusetts, *ed. W.H. Whitmore (Boston,
1889); the second selection on the somnolent sinner is taken from Increase Mather's* Practical Truths Tending to Promote the Power of
Godliness *(Boston, 1682), pp. 209-212; the final selection is the
dramatic catalogue of felt transgressions that a reforming synod of
New England clergymen issued in 1680, a typically Puritan document that can be found in Williston Walker,* Creeds and Platforms of
Congregationalism *(New York, 1893), pp. 426-432.*

SABBATH

*Upon information of sundry Abuses and Misdemeanours Com-
mitted by divers Persons on the Lords day, not onely by Children
playing in the streets, and other places, but by Youths, Mayds, and
other persons, both strangers and others, uncivilly walking in the
streets and fields, travailing from town to town, going on Ship-board,
frequenting common houses, and other places to drink, Sport, or
otherwise to mispend that precious time, which thing tends much to
the dishonour of God, the Reproach of Religion, greiving the soules
of Gods servants, and the Prophanation of his holy Sabbath, the
Sanctification whereof, is sometimes put for all duties, immediately
respecting the Service of God conteined in the first Table. It is
therefore Ordered by this Court and the Authority thereof, That no
Children, Youths, Mayds or other Persons, shall Transgress in the like*

kind on penalty of being Reputed *great provokers of the high displeasure of the Almighty GOD*, and further incurs the penalty hereafter expressed, *viz*. That the Parents and Governours of all children above seven yeares old, (not that we approve young children in evill) for the first offence in that kind, upon due proof before any Magistrate, Commissioner or Select man of the Town, where such offence shall be committed, shall be *admonished*; for a second offence upon due proof as aforesaid shall pay as a fine *five shillings*, and for a third offence upon due proof as aforesaid, *ten shillings*; and if they shall again offend in that kind, they shall be presented to the County Court, who shall augment punishment according to the merit of the fact. And for all youths and mayds above fourteen yeares old, and all elder persons whatsoever, that shall offend, and be convict as aforesaid, either for *playing, uncivel walking, drinking, travailing* from Town to Town, *going on ship-board, sporting*, or any way *mispending* that presious time, shall for the first Offence be *Admonished*, upon due proof as aforesayd, for a second Offence shall pay as a fine *five shillings*, & for the third offence *ten shillings*, and if any shall further Offend that way, they shall be bound over to the next County Court, who shall *augment punishment* according to the nature of the Offence, and if any be unable or unwilling to pay the aforesaid fines, they shall be whiped by the Constable not exceeding *Five Stripes*, for *Ten Shillings* fine and this to be understood of such Offences, as shall be Committed, during the Day Light of the Lords Day. [1653]

2. *Whereas by too sad Experience, it is observed, the Sun being set, both every Saturday, and on the Lords Day, young people and others take Liberty to walk* & Sport themselves in the streets or fields *in the several Townes of this Jurisdiction, to the dishonour of God and the disturbance of others in their Religious exercises, and too frequently repair to publick houses of entertainment and there sit Drinking, all which tends not onely to the hindring of due preparation for the Sabbath, but as much as in them lyeth, renders the Ordinances of God unprofitable, and threatens the rooting out of the Power of Godlines, and procuring the wrath* & Judgment of God upon *us* & our posterity for prevention whereof. It is Ordered by this Court and the Authority thereof, That if any person or persons henceforth, either on the Saturday night, or on the Lords day night, after the Sun is set, shall be found sporting in the streets or fields of any town in this Jurisdiction, Drinking, or being in any house of publick entertainment (unless strangers or Sojourners in their Lodgings) and can-

not give a satisfactory Reason to such Magistrate or Commishoner, in the severall Towns, as shall have the Cognizance thereof. Every such Person so found Complained of and Prooved Transgressing, shall pay *Five shillings* for every such Transgression or Suffer *Corporall* Punishment, as Authority Aforesayd shall Determine. [1658]

SLEEPING AT SERMONS

Instr. 1. *We may here take notice that the nature of man is wofully corrupted and depraved*, else they would not be so apt to sleep when the precious Truths of God are dispensed in his Name, Yea, and men are more apt to sleep then, than at another time. Some woful Creatures, have been so wicked as to profess they have gone to hear Sermons on purpose, that so they might sleep, finding themselves at such times much disposed that way. This argueth as Satans malice, so the great corruption and depravation of the nature of men, whence it is that they are inclined unto evil, and indisposed to the thing that good is. Yea, some will sit and sleep under the best Preaching in the World. When *Paul* was alive, there was not a better Preacher upon the Earth then he. *Austin* had three wishes: one was, that (if the Lord had seen meet) he might see Christ in the flesh: his second wish was, that he might have seen *Paul in the Pulpit;* but notwithstanding *Pauls* being so excellent a Preacher, there were some that could sit and sleep under his Ministry. When Soul-melting Sermons are Preached about Christ the Saviour, about the pardon of sin, about the glory of Heaven, there are some that will sleep under them. When soul-awakening Sermons are Preached enough to make rocks to rend and to bleed; when the word falls down from Heaven like Thunder, the voice of the Lord therein being very powerful and full of Majesty, able to break the Cedars of *Lebanon*, and to make the wilderness to shake; yet some will sit and sleep under it: such is the woful corruption and desperate hardness of the hearts of the Children of men.

Instr. 2. *Hence see, that there is great danger in those things which men are apt to look upon as little sins, yea as no sins at all*.

As for sleeping at Sermons, some look upon it as no sin; others account it a *peccadillo*, a sin not worth taking notice of, or the troubling themselves about. But my Text sheweth that danger and death is in it. We have solemn Instances in the Scripture, concerning those that have lost their lives, because they have been guilty of such miscarriages, as carnal reason will say are but little sins. When there was a man that gathered a few sticks upon the Sabbath day, he was put to death for it; and yet men would be apt to think his sin was not (though indeed it was) very great. Men account it a small matter to add something of their own to the worship of God: but when *Nadab* and *Abihu* did so, *there went out fire from the Lord*, and consumed them to death. Wher *Vzzah* a good man, did with a pious intention touch the Ark, (which he being no Priest should not have done) *God smote him for his Error, that he dyed by the Ark of God*. Behold! the severity of God, and let us tremble at it. Common sins, which almost every one is guilty of, are accounted small iniquities; but there is exceeding danger in following a multitude to do evil. Sins of Omission are esteemed small, but mens Souls may be thrown into the fire and burned for ever, not only for bearing evil fruit, but because they do not bring forth good fruit, *Mat*. 3. 10. At the last day the Son of God will pronounce a Sentence of eternal death upon thousands of Millions, because they have omitted these and those duties which he required and expected from them. Sinful words are looked upon as small evils by many. How common is it for persons to say, *what shall we be made offenders for a word?* abusing that Scripture which reproveth those that make others offenders for speaking good and faithful words. But doth not the Scripture say, *by thy words thou shalt be condemned, Mat*. 12. 37. Corrupt communications, obscene discourses, unclean lascivious speeches, discover the persons that delight in them to be amongst the number of those that shall (without Repentance) be condemned at the day of *Judgement*, yet there are some that make light of them. Thus concerning those words which some call *Petty Oathes;* some are so profanely ignorant as to think, that they may Swear by *their Faith and Troth*, and that there is no great hurt or danger in it. But there is danger of no less than Damnation for these seemingly little sins, if men shall allow themselves therein, notwithstanding the Commandment of God to the contrary. See the word of the Lord to this purpose, *Jam*. 5. 12. *But above all things Swear not,* (i.e. vainly, or except duely called therunto) *neither by Heaven, neither by the Earth, neither by any other Oath*, therefore not by your Faith or Troth, *lest you fall into condemnation*.

Again sinful thoughts are esteemed small evils; but I must tell you

QUESTION I

What are the evils that have provoked the Lord to bring His judgments on New England?

Answer. . . .

That God hath a controversy with His New England people is undeniable, the Lord having written His displeasure in dismal characters against us. Though personal afflictions do oftentimes come only or chiefly for probation, yet as to public judgments it is not wont to be so; especially when by a continued series of providence, the Lord doth appear and plead against His people. 2 Sam. 21:1. As with us it hath been from year to year. Would the Lord have whetted His glittering sword, and His hand have taken hold on judgment? Would He have sent such a mortal contagion like a besom of destruction in the midst of us? Would He have said, Sword! go through the land, and cut off man and beast? Or would He have kindled such devouring fires, and made such fearful desolations in the earth, if He had not been angry? It is not for nothing that the merciful God, who doth not willingly afflict nor grieve the children of men, hath done all these things unto us; yea and sometimes with a cloud hath covered Himself, that our prayer should not pass through. And although 'tis possible that the Lord may contend with us partly on account of secret unobserved sins (Josh. 7:11, 12; 2 King. 17:9; Psal. 90:8), in which respect, a deep and most serious inquiry into the causes of His controversy ought to be attended. Nevertheless, it is sadly evident that there are visible, manifest evils, which without doubt the Lord is provoked by. For,

I. There is a great and visible decay of the power of godliness amongst many professors in these churches. It may be feared that there is in too many spiritual and heart apostasy from God, whence communion with Him in the ways of His worship, especially in secret is much neglected, and whereby men cease to know and fear and love and trust in Him, but take up their contentment and satisfaction in something else. This was the ground and bottom of the Lord's controversy with His people of old. Psal. 78:8, 37, and 81:11; Jer. 2:5, 11, 13. And with His people under the New Testament also. Rev. 2:4, 5.

II. The pride that doth abound in New England testifies against us. Hos. 5:5; Ezek. 7:10. Both spiritual pride, Zeph. 3:11. Whence two great evils and provocations have proceeded and prevailed amongst us.

1. A refusing to be subject to order according to divine appointment, Numb. 16:3; 1 Pet. 5:5.

2. Contention. Prov. 13:10. An evil that is most eminently against the solemn charge of the Lord Jesus, Joh. 13:34, 35. And that for which God hath by severe judgments punished His people, both in former and latter ages. This malady hath been very general in the country; we have therefore cause to fear that the wolves which God in His holy providence hath let loose upon us have been sent to chastise His sheep for their dividings and strayings one from another, and that the wars and fightings which have proceeded from the lust of pride in special, have been punished with the sword Jam. 4:1; Job. 19:29.

Yea, and pride in respect to apparel hath greatly abounded. Servants and the poorer sort of people are notoriously guilty in the matter, who (too generally) go above their estates and degrees, thereby transgressing the laws both of God and man, Math. 11:8. Yea, it is a sin that even the light of nature, and laws of civil nations have condemned. 1 Cor. 11:14. Also, many, not of the meaner sort, have offended God by strange apparel, not becoming serious Christians, especially in these days of affliction and misery, wherein the Lord calls upon men to put off their ornaments, Exod. 33:5; Jer. 4:30. A sin which brings wrath upon the greatest that shall be found guilty of it, Zeph. 1:8; with Jer. 52:13. Particularly, the Lord hath threatened to visit with sword and sickness and with loathsome diseases for this very sin. Isai. 3:16.

III. Inasmuch as it was in a more peculiar manner with respect to the second Commandment, that our fathers did follow the Lord into this wilderness, whilst it was a land not sown, we may fear that the breaches of that Commandment are some part of the Lord's controversy with New England. Church fellowship and other divine institutions are greatly neglected. Many of the rising generation are not mindful of that which their baptism doth engage them unto, viz. to use utmost endeavors that they may be fit for, and so partake in, all the holy ordinances of the Lord Jesus. Math. 28:20. There are too many that with profane Esau slight spiritual privileges. Nor is there so much of discipline extended towards the children of the covenant, as we are generally agreed ought to be done. On the other hand, humane inventions, and will-worship have been set up even in

Jerusalem. Men have set up their thresholds by God's threshold, and their posts by His post. Quakers are false worshipers; and such Anabaptists as have risen up amongst us, in opposition to the churches of the Lord Jesus, receiving into their society those that have been for scandal delivered unto Satan, yea, and improving those as administrators of holy things, who have been (as doth appear) justly under Church censures, do no better than set up an altar against the Lord's altar. Wherefore it must needs be provoking to God, if these things be not duly and fully testified against by everyone in their several capacities respectively. Josh. 22:19; 2 King. 23:13; Ezek. 43:8; Psal. 99:8; Hos. 11:6.

IV. The holy and glorious name of God hath been polluted and profaned amongst us, more especially:

1. By oaths and imprecations in ordinary discourse; yea, and it is too common a thing for men in a more solemn way to swear unnecessary oaths, whenas it is a breach of the third Commandment so to use the blessed name of God. And many (if not the most) of those that swear consider not the rule of an oath. Jer. 4:2. So that we may justly fear that because of swearing the land mourns, Jer. 23:10.

2. There is great profaneness in respect of irreverent behavior in the solemn worship of God. It is a frequent thing for men (though not necessitated thereunto by any infirmity) to sit in prayer time, and some with their heads almost covered, and to give way to their own sloth and sleepiness, when they should be serving God with attention and intention, under the solemn dispensation of His ordinances. We read but of one man in the scripture that slept at a sermon, and that sin hath like to have cost him his life, Act. 20:9.

V. There is much sabbath-breaking. Since there are multitudes that do profanely absent themselves or theirs from the public worship of God, on His holy day, especially in the most populous places the land, and many under pretense of differing apprehensions about the beginning of the sabbath do not keep a seventh part of time holy unto the Lord, as the fourth Commandment requireth, walking abroad, and traveling (not merely on the account of worshiping God in the solemn assemblies of His people or to attend works of necessity or mercy), being a common practice on the sabbath day, which is contrary unto that rest enjoined by the Commandment. Yea, some that attend their particular servile callings and employments after the sabbath is begun, or before it is ended. Worldly, unsuitable discourses are very common upon the Lord's day, contrary to the scripture which requireth that men should not on holy times find their own pleasure, nor speak their own words, Isai. 58:13. Many that do not take care so to dispatch their worldly businesses, that they may be free and fit for the duties of the sabbath, and that do (if not wholly neglect) after a careless, heartless manner perform the duties that concern the sanctification of the sabbath. This brings wrath, fires, and other judgments upon a professing people, Neh. 3:17, 18; Jer. 17:27.

VI. As to what concerns families and the government thereof, there is much amiss. There are many families that do not pray to God constantly, morning and evening, and many more wherein the scriptures are not daily read, that so the word of Christ might dwell richly with them. Some (and too many) houses that are full of ignorance and profaneness, and these not duly inspected, for which cause wrath may come upon others round about them, as well as upon themselves. Josh. 22:20; Jer. 5:7, and 10:25. And many householders who profess religion do not cause all that are within their gates to become subject unto good order, as ought to be. Exod. 20:10. Nay, children and servants that are not kept in due subjection, their masters, and parents especially, being sinfully indulgent towards them. This is a sin which brings great judgments, as we see in Eli's and David's family. In this respect, Christians in this land, have become too like unto the Indians, and then we need not wonder if the Lord hath afflicted us by them. Sometimes a sin is discerned by the instrument that providence doth punish with. Most of the evils that abound amongst us proceed from defects as to family government.

VII. Inordinate passions. Sinful heats and hatreds, and that amongst church-members themselves, who abound with evil surmisings, uncharitable and unrighteous censures, backbitings, hearing and telling tales, few that remember and duly observe the rule, with an angry countenance to drive away the talebearer; reproachful and reviling expressions, sometimes to or of one another. Hence lawsuits are frequent, brother going to law with brother, and provoking and abusing one another in public courts of judicature, to the scandal of their holy profession, Isai. 58:4; 1 Cor. 6:6, 7. And in managing the discipline of Christ, some (and too many) are acted by their passions and prejudices more than by a spirit of love and faithfulness towards their brother's soul, which things are as against the law of Christ, so dreadful violations of the church covenant, made in the presence of God.

VIII. There is much intemperance. The heathenish and idolatrous practice of health-drinking is too frequent. That shameful iniquity of sinful drinking is become too general a provocation. Days of training, and other public solemnities have been abused in this respect. And not only English but Indians have been debauched by those that call themselves Christians, who have put their bottles to them, and made them drunk also. This is a crying sin, and the more aggravated in that the first planters of this colony did (as is in the patent expressed) come into this land with a design to convert the heathen unto Christ, but if instead of that, they be taught wickedness, which before they were never guilty of, the Lord may well punish us by them. Moreover, the sword, sickness, poverty, and almost all the judgments which have been upon New England, are mentioned in the scripture as the woeful fruit of *that sin*. Isai. 5:11, 12, and 28:1, 2, and 56:9, 12; Prov. 23:21, 29, 30, and 21:17; Hos. 7:5, and 2:8, 9. There are more temptations and occasions unto *that sin*, publicly allowed of, than any necessity doth require; the proper end of taverns, etc., being for the entertainment of strangers, which if they were improved to that end only, a far less number would suffice. But it is a common practice for town-dwellers, yea and church-members, to frequent public houses, and there to misspend precious time, unto the dishonor of the gospel, and the scandalizing of others, who are by such examples induced to sin against God. In which respect, for church-members to be unnecessarily in such houses is sinful, scandalous, and provoking to God. 1 Cor. 8:9, 10; Rom. 14:21; Math. 17:27, and 18:7.

And there are other heinous breaches of the seventh Commandment. Temptations thereunto are become too common, viz., such as immodest apparel, Prov. 7:10, laying out of hair, borders, naked necks and arms, or, which is more abominable, naked breasts, and mixed dancings, light behavior and expressions, sinful company-keeping with light and vain persons, unlawful gaming, an abundance of idleness, which brought ruinating judgment upon Sodom, and much more upon Jerusalem (Ezek. 16:49) and doth sorely threaten New England unless effectual remedies be thoroughly and timeously applied.

IX. There is much want of truth amongst men. Promise-breaking is a common sin, for which New England doth hear ill abroad in the world. And the Lord hath threatened for that transgression to give His people into the hands of their enemies, and that their dead bodies should be for meat unto the fowls of heaven and to the beasts of the earth; which judgments have been verified upon us, Jer. 34:18, 20. And false reports have been too common; yea, walking with slanders and reproaches, and that sometimes against the most faithful and eminent servants of God. The Lord is not wont to suffer such iniquity to pass unpunished. Jer. 9:4, 5; Numb. 16:41.

X. Inordinate affection to the world. Idolatry is a God-provoking, judgment-procuring sin. And covetousness is idolatry. Eph. 5:5. There hath been in many professors an insatiable desire after land and worldly accommodations, yea, so as to forsake churches and ordinances, and to live like heathen, only that so they might have elbow-room enough in the world. Farms and merchandising have been preferred before the things of God. In this respect, the interest of New England seemeth to be changed. We differ from other outgoings of our nation in that it was not any worldly consideration that brought our fathers into this wilderness, but religion, even that so they might build a sanctuary unto the Lord's name; whereas now religion is made subservient unto worldly interests. Such iniquity causeth war to be in the gates, and cities to be burnt up. Judg. 8:5; Math. 22:5, 7. Wherefore, we cannot but solemnly bear witness against that practice of settling plantations without any ministry amongst them, which is to prefer the world before the gospel. When Lot did forsake the Land of Canaan, and the church which was in Abraham's family, that so he might have better worldly accommodations in Sodom, God fired him out of all, and he was constrained to leave his goodly pastures, which his heart (though otherwise a good man) was too much set upon. Moreover, that many are under the prevailing power of the sin of worldliness is evident:

1. From that oppression which the land groaneth under. There are some traders who sell their goods at excessive rates, day-laborers and mechanics are unreasonable in their demands. Yea, there have been those that have dealt deceitfully and oppressively towards the heathen amongst whom we live, whereby they have been scandalized and prejudiced against the name of Christ. The scripture doth frequently threaten judgments for the sin of oppression, and in special the oppressing sword cometh as a just punishment for that evil. Ezek. 7:11, and 22:15; Prov. 28:8; Isai. 5:7.

2. It is also evident that men are under the prevailing power of a worldly spirit; by their strait-handedness as to public concernments. God by a continued series of providence, for many years one after

another, hath been blasting the fruits of the earth in a great measure, and this year more abundantly. Now if we search the scriptures, we shall find that when the Lord hath been provoked to destroy the fruits of the earth, either by noxious creatures, or by his own immediate hand in blastings or droughts or excessive rains (all which judgments we have experience of), it hath been mostly for this sin of strait-handedness with reference unto public and pious concerns, Hag. 1:9; Mal. 3:8, 9, 11. As when people's hearts and hands are enlarged upon these accounts, God hath promised (and is wont in his faithful providence to do accordingly) to bless with outward plenty and prosperity, Prov. 3:9, 10; Mal. 3:10; I Cor. 9:6, 8, 10; 2 Chron. 31:10. So on the other hand, when men withhold more than is meet, the Lord sends impoverishing judgments upon them, Prov. 11:24.

XI. There hath been opposition unto the work of reformation. Although the Lord hath been calling upon us, not only by the voice of His servants, but by awful judgments, that we should return unto Him who hath been smiting us, and notwithstanding all the good laws that are established for the suppression of growing evils, yet men *will not* return every one from his evil way. There hath been great incorrigibleness under lesser judgments. Sin and sinners have many advocates. They that have been zealous in bearing witness against the sins of the times have been reproached, and other ways discouraged, which argueth an heart unwilling to reform. Hence the Lord's controversy is not yet done, but His hand is stretched out still, Lev. 26:23, 24; Isai. 12:13.

XII. A public spirit is greatly wanting in the most of men. Few that are of Nehemiah's spirit, Neh. 5:15. All seek their own, not the things that are Jesus Christ's, serving themselves upon Christ and His holy ordinances. Matters appertaining to the Kingdom of God are either not at all regarded or not in the first place. Hence schools of learning and other public concerns are in a languishing state. Hence also are unreasonable complaints and murmurings because of public charges, which is a great sin and a private selfseeking spirit is one of those evils that renders the last times perilous, 2 Tim. 3:1.

XIII. There are sins against the gospel, whereby the Lord hath been provoked. Christ is not prized and embraced in all His offices and ordinances as ought to be. Manna hath been loathed, the pleasant land despised, Psal. 106:24. Though the gospel and covenant of grace call upon men to repent, yet there are multitudes that refuse to repent, when the Lord doth vouchsafe them time and means. No sins provoke the Lord more than impenitency and unbelief, Jer. 8:6; Zech. 7:11, 12, 13; Heb. 3:17, 18; Rev. 2:21, 22. There is great unfruitfulness under the means of grace, and that brings the most desolating judgments Isai. 5:4; Math. 3:10, and 21:43. 13.

Finally, there are several considerations which seem to evidence that the evils mentioned are the matters of the Lord's controversy:

1. In that (though not as to all) as to most of them they are sins which many are guilty of,

2. Sins which have been acknowledged before the Lord on days of humiliation appointed by authority, and yet not reformed.

3. Many of them not punished (and some of them not punishable) by men, therefore the Lord Himself doth punish for them.

VII. DEATH

In the uncertainty of life is the certainty of death. How long could the New England colonists expect to live? Could men expect to live longer than women? Why? What did the faithful Puritans hope for at death? Did they have any assurances? What was the minister's role at the approach of death? How were New England funerals conducted? For whom were they primarily intended? What was the significance of giving rings, gloves, and scarves at funerals? What were the benefits of attending funerals? What was the religious significance of funerals for the Puritans? What was the popular conception of the Day of Judgement? Who sat on the right hand of God? the left? (Recall the position of boy and girl children *in utero*.) What were their respective rewards? How did their conception of Judgement Day affect the living behavior of the Puritans?

Death punches no timeclock, but in most New England communities people died with a certain regularity. John Demos has calculated the incidence of mortality among the people of 17th-century Plymouth in A Little Commonwealth *(New York, 1970), pp. 192-193. (See also Tables 1 and 2 for infant mortality.)*

Table 7:

LIFE EXPECTANCY IN PLYMOUTH COLONY

Age	Men	Women
21	69.1	62.4
30	70.0	64.7
40	71.2	69.7
50	73.7	73.4
60	76.3	76.8
70	79.9	80.7
80	85.1	86.7

Note: The figures in the left-hand column are the control points, that is, a twenty-one-year-old man might expect to live to age 69.2, a thirty-year-old to 70.0, and so forth. The sample on which this table is based comprises a total of 645 persons.

Table 8:

DEATHS ARRANGED ACCORDING TO AGE (PLYMOUTH COLONY)

Age Group	Men (percentages)	Women (percentages)
22-29	1.6	5.9
30-39	3.6	12.0
40-49	7.8	12.0
50-59	10.2	10.9
60-69	18.0	14.9
70-79	30.5	20.7
80-89	22.4	16.0
90 or over	5.9	7.6

Note: The figures in columns two and three represent the percentages of the men and women in the sample who died between the ages indicated in column one. The sample is the same as in Table 7.

Man is never more alone than when he approaches death. It is then that most people search for comfort and courage, just as Mrs. Samuel Forbush of Westborough, Massachusetts turned to the Rev. Ebenezer Parkman. Her somewhat unusual deathbed scene is taken from the Proceedings *of the American Antiquarian Society, vol. 71 (1961), pp. 186-191.*

1727: **21 APRIL.**

Sometime after Sun down Lieutenant Forbush came and requested me to go down to See his Wife who they thought was drawing near her End and wanted to See Me. I went down. When I Entered I Said Mrs. Forbush I am Sorry to See you So ill; I am come at your Desire; which way can I become the most Serviceable to you? She reply'd She was under apprehension of the approach of Death and she could not but be under fears on So great an Occasion. Upon which I proceeded to enquire into the grounds of her Fears telling withal that I should endeavour to remove them and (receiving Some very generall answers) to promote the matter the more readily I began to Say Something concerning true Repentance, universal Obedience and the unfeigned Love of God and to the People of God which finding in her might Shew to her the Truth of Grace to be wrought in her, which being demonstrated must necessarily make all things bright and clear and comfortable. But this process I managed in such an easy and familiar manner as this following.

1. I am hoping (Mrs. Forbush) you have freely repented of any sin that you have known your Self guilty of. She answer'd that She trusted she had, and was heartily willing to, of all that she had been chargeable with that she had not particularly known of, etc.

2. You have told me heretofore that you have us'd your utmost to keep the Commands of God universally but especially now Since you have openly dedicated your Self to God, and join'd your Self to the Communion of the Lords people and waited upon Christ Table I conclude you have much ground for Satisfaction and Comfort. (You Should have if you have Sincerely and uprightly done your Duty). To which she [said] It has indeed been a Comfort to me and I am now

glad that I have not that work to reproach my Self with the commission of, (or in these words) I am glad havn't that work to do now (having some reference I believe to the Trouble that many have been in at such an hour that they had never obey'd the Comand of Christ.) etc., etc., etc.

3. Well, Mrs. Forbush but to let you see things more plainly Still. Let Us a little further enquire. Don't you find in you Such a Love to God as has made you both repent of Sin and Obey his Comands from a Desire of his Glory? etc. etc.

But to find out some further proof of all this and to have some stronger evidence of your Love to God and Christ, have you a pure love to the Godly; do you love the Disciples of Christ, those that you think bear the Image of God unfeignedly?

She. I hope really that I do.

N. B. Mr. Thomas Forbush and wife, Captain Byles and wife, and Jedediah How were in the Room, besides the family. But the person being look'd upon as near expiring I thought not to thrust those persons So well acquainted with the woman, as nearer She has not (except one), out of the room, and Seeing my discourse was generall and what anyone might hear. Yet when under any of those heads any particular private matters have occurr'd it has then been usuall with me to desire the Company to withdraw. But here I apprehended would be such things spoken as might be very profitable and suitable for all that heard, as I concluded these near Relatives were gratify'd not a little by them. However, upon some account or other it Seems Old Mr. Forbush is displeased and tho at the most awfull time when every thought was profoundly Serious and solemn Yet he thinks fit to [illegible] upon us in a sad passionate manner upon the last Sentence, spoken thus. Sir, We are grown folks. I turned about in great Surprize and calmly looking upon him and then as calmly Speaking asked what he had said. He repeated the Same words as before. I asked him what then? (Now raising my Self up in my Chair) why then (says he) we understand these things already have read in the Bible and Some other Books, and ourselves know these things being grown folks and come into years. Here up I Spoke the words followng (his Wife, his Sisters, especially the apprehended Dying person besought him not to open his mouth any further, they being astonished as well as I and the woman declaring it much to her Comfort and benefit that I had proceeded as I had and that it was the End of her sending for me, etc.). Mr. Forbush, I am astonish'd at such an interruption at such a season, when I come upon my Commission and Charge to minister in the name of God to a Servant of his ready to leave the world, etc., etc. Says he, If I had been in your place I would not have asked Such Questions. I reply'd in defence of them. He Said Mr. Breck would not ask Such. I answer'd I was not now to enquire what Mr. Breck would ask, but I was able to affirm that the most Learned, the most pious and the most Judicious ministers would. I therewith pray'd him to Say which were improper and wherein. He appear'd not able to tell so much as what any one Question was that I had asked. Well, Said I, Seeing you won't or can't tell me which, etc., I'll endeavour to recollect all that I have said, though I did not Study before I came down what I should say, nor had I time; neither did I confine my Self strictly to any Method but Said what I thought of the greatest weight in the Case before me. I then recapitulated and demanded as I went along what exceptions he had to make and wherein they were so grossly injudicious as to be foundation enough for his So Strange interposition. 1. He Suppos'd She had repented before now and she had examin'd her Self before this time o'Day often and often no doubt. And then I had liv'd in the house and knew the woman long ago. So that I had no need to ask Questions now. Besides I had or Should have ask'd her when She was admitted into the Church. Truly, said he, if it was my wife you Should not have asked her whether she had repented of her sins. We hope She has done it long ago. To which I Said, This Person I knew So Well as that I Saw no danger from my asking generall Questions. She has had nothing Scandalous in all her Life that I know of, neither could any one think that I desir'd to rake into all the particulars of her past conversation in the world and managements in the Familie (not but that If I had made Such enquries She might I believe have produc'd what would have been very instructing). Were I examining a person that had been notoriously vicious and demanding a particular confession and before So many witnesses it had been another thing; but I have been endeavouring to assist this person in preparing actually to give up her account to the great Judge, and though she may have view'd it numberless times and we may have review'd and examin'd it together yet now at the awfull juncture before delivering it into his hands we act most wisely to look all over as carefully as possible to find out whatever escapes or flaws there may be, Since it can never be done after, throughout Eternity, and Eternity depends upon this account.

Mr. Forbush those Questions appear injudicious to you; yet they are so far from being a reflection upon your Sister that the most advanc'd Christian that is on Earth won't Scruple to ask them and they are the very questions therefore that the gravest and profoundest Divines in the Christian Church do put in these Cases, etc. etc.

2. You ask (Say'd he) whether she had not comfort in her having bccn at the Sacrament. How needless that question. What do you think She went to it for, Sir? I admire at you Mr. Forbush. Your Sister's End was to testifie her Obedience to the Command of Christ, and to obtain of her Lord Divine Grace and Support under all Troubles and difficulties, to Engage Gods mercifull presence in a time of Extremity, especially when Death approaches. She has been I Say, for these great and important things and now when She needs them most of all I ask whether she has got her Errand and how she is Sure She has these things and This is impertinent, etc., etc.

3. And You asked whether She lov'd the Godly? What a Question that is! I know what you mean whether She loves all that Appear professedly to be Christians. I havn't a Charity for everybody because they make a profession. There is some that I know of that I won't have a Charity for tho they have join'd to the Church. To which I rejoin'd Mr. Forbush in trying whether true Grace be in the heart love to Christ's Disciples is always enquir'd into. I doubted not but your Sister doth So, yet it is ask'd to make all things as clear and fair as possible. By Christ's Disciples I mean the Same as Saint John doth by the Brethren by which are understood all that any way bear the Image and Resemblence of Christ, and Mr. Forbush notwithstanding what you have last Said as to your Charity I'll tell you mine is So extensive that there is not a person in all Westboro but I would charitably hope he may be a subject for the Divine Grace to work upon. Well, he would not, etc. It was time I should do what I could for the woman. I told him he had prevented me and unfitted me, etc., but I turn'd about and went on. Mr. Forbush ask'd I'd forgive him if he had said anything wrong but he thought he would not ask Such questions. So that I So far lost my labour with him. I told him if he was So much disturb'd about them, I would submit them to the Judgement to whatsoever ministers in the country he should Choose. I pray'd him to consider his sister. He was willing with all Saying that he knew not how soon he should need me on the Same account and

therefore again desire me to forgive his bluntness, but yet He could not desire me if ever I should to ask him such sort of Questions. Thus did he in a strange manner keep up the flame by throwing in oil when he pretended to cast in water to quench it. No, Mr. Forbush Said I with some earnestness, I'm afraid you would not care that I should deal feelingly with your soul. I now told him of my being oblig'd in Conscience to do my utmost for persons when as his Sister, etc. I shall take no further notice of the Strange reply he made me nor the long discourse he further occasion'd. I was griev'd heartily to See So much of his ignorance and passions. It grew very late. It was well the woman (it may be through her fright) was reviv'd. We came into So amicable a Composition as to go to prayer and we parted Friends. But both my Head and heart were full. It was Twelve when I got home. Sister Ruth discern'd my Trouble. I went to bed but could not Sleep for a long time. I beseach God to quicken me hereby in my work, and make me more diligent to accomplish my Self lest I meet with worse trialls than this. I remember and would take notice of it that the Suddenness and lateness of Lieutenant's coming for me prevented my usual address to heaven before such Ministrations. I would be humbled for my Sin and take the Punishment God inflicted for it.

Every culture takes leave of its dead in distinctive ways. Samuel Sewall witnessed the Puritan way of dying from the hub of New England society. The passages from his diary are taken from the Collections *of the Massachusetts Historical Society, fifth series, vols. 6-7.*

July, 25th 1700. Went to the Funeral of Mrs. Sprague, being invited by a good pair of Gloves.
1700: Novr. 30th. My Aunt Quinsey dieth of the Jaundice befor break of day.
Thorsday, xr. 5th. 1700. Sam. and I ride to the Funeral of Aunt Eli. Quinsey. Because of the Porrige of snow, Bearers—Mr. Torrey, Fisk, Thacher, I, Danforth, Wilson, Bechar—rid to the Grave, alighting a little before they came there. Mourners, Cous. Edward and his Sister rid first, then Mrs. Ana Quinsey, widow, behind Mr. Allen; and cous. Ruth Hunt behind her Husband; then Sam. and I. None of the Gookings there. Mr. Torrey prayed. Bearers had Rings and Wash-Lether Gloves. I had Gloves and a Ring. Cous. Edmund

invited us; for I lodg'd there all night, with Mr. Torrey, Sam. with his Cousin. All else went home. Cousin Savil was at Weymouth and came not. Funeral about 4. p.m.

1701: Jany. 15th. Sam. and I set forward. Brother Northend meets us. Visit Aunt Northend, Mr. Payson. With Brother and sister we set forward for Newbury: where we find that day apointed for the Funeral: twas a very pleasant Comfortable day.

Bearers, Jno Kent of the Island, Lt Cutting Noyes, Deacon William Noyes, Mr. Peter Tappan, Capt. Henry Somersby, Mr. Joseph Woodbridge. I follow'd the Bier single. Then Brother Sewall and sister Jane, Brother Short and his wife, Brother Moodey and his wife, Brother Northend and his wife, Brother Tapan and sister Sewall, Sam. and cous. Hañah Tapan. Mr. Payson of Rowley, Mr. Clark, Minister of Excester, were there. Col. Pierce, Major Noyes &c. Cous. John, Richard and Betty Dumer. Went abt 4. p.m. Nathan Bricket taking in hand to fill the Grave, I said, Forbear a little, and suffer me to say That amidst our bereaving sorrows We have the Comfort of beholding this Saint put into the rightfull possession of that Happiness of Living desir'd and dying Lamented. She liv'd comendably Four and Fifty years with her dear Husband, and my dear Father: And she could not well brook the being divided from him at her death; which is the cause of our taking leave of her in this place. She was a true and constant Lover of Gods Word, Worship, and Saints: And she always, with a patient cheerfullness, submitted to the divine Decree of providing Bread for her self and others in the sweat of her Brows. And now her infinitely Gracious and Bountiful Master has promoted her to the Honor of higher Employments, fully and absolutely discharged from all maner of Toil, and Sweat. My honoured and beloved Friends and Neighbours! My dear Mother never thought much of doing the most frequent and homely offices of Love for me; and lavish'd away many Thousands of Words upon me, before I could return one word in Answer: And therefore I ask and hope that none will be offended that I have now ventured to speak one word in her behalf; when shee her self is become speechless. Made a Motion with my hand for the filling of the Grave. Note, I could hardly speak for passion and Tears. Mr. Tappan pray'd with us in the evening. I lodg'd at sister Gerrishes with Joseph. Brother and Sam. at Br. Tapans. Jany. 16th. The two Brothers and four sisters being together, we took Leave by singing of the 90th Psalm, from the 8th. to the 15th. verse inclusively. Mr. Brown, the Scholar, was present. Set out abt 11. for Ipswich, got time enough to hear Mr. Rogers preach the Lecture from Luke 1. 76. about ministerial preparation for Christ. Sung the nine first verses of the 132. Psalm. Mr. Rogers prai'd for the prisoner of death, the Newbury woman who was there in her chains. This is the last Sermon preached in the old Meeting-house. Eat Roost Fowl at Crompton's. Delivered a Letter to the Widow Hale; got very comfortably over the Ferry to Brothers whether Mr. Hirst quickly came to welcome us and invite us to dine or breakfast next day, which we did, the morning being cold: Visited Madam Bradstreet and Major Brown, and told them of the death of their fellow-passenger. Rec'd me very courteously. Took horse about one p.m. Baited at Lewis's; Stop'd at Govr Usher's to pay him a visit. He and his Lady being from home, we pass'd on, and got to Charlestown about Sun-set, very comfortably. Found all well at home through the Goodness of God.

1703: Decr 11. Poor little Hull Sewall dies in Mr. Phips's house at Muddy-River about 6. in the evening, of Convulsions. About 8. at night the Govr sends us word of it. Decr 14th. Corps is brought to Town in the Governours Slay. Decr 15. is born to our Tomb, and set upon a Box that his great Grandfathers Bones now put into it at Williams's desire, some being wash'd out. On the Box is made with Nails, 1683. Bearers were Mr. Nathan Oliver and David Stoddard.— Govrs Lady and my wife rode in the Coach. Son and daughter followed the little Corps in Mourning: then Grandfathers, Joseph and Hannah, Mr. Hirst and his wife. Several of the Council here, and Mr. Cotton Mather, Mr. Nehemiah Walter. Provided new oak Plank for the entrance of the Tomb. Madam Leverett and Usher there. Gave no Gloves.

1706: Decr 20, *feria sexta*, very Rainy day; Mr. Winthrop, Russel, Elisha Hutchinson, Em Hutchinson, Mr. Foster, Sewall, Townsend, Walley, Bromfield, Belchar Dine at the Governour's, Mr. Secretary. Go in Coaches. After Diner I visit Mr. Bayley; Is in great Extremity, Paroxisms return in about 1/2 hour; seem'd to desire death; and yet once I took notice that he breath'd after some space and recovery of strength before went hence: leave all to God's unerring Providence. He told me he heard Sister Short was dangerously sick: heard of by Jona Emery. Came home to the Meeting at Mr. Bromfield's, Mr. Williams of Deerfield preach'd: very Rainy, and dirty under foot. When came home, or a little after, had a Letter brought me of the

Death of Sister Shortt the 18th. Inst. which was very surprising to me. Half are now dead. The Lord fit me for my Departure. Decr. 21. Not having other Mourning, I look'd out a pair of Mourning Gloves. An hour or 2 after, Mr. Sergeant, sent me and my wife Gloves; mine are so little I cant wear them. See Jan. 20. 1705-6. Mr. Cooper's Son brought them, I gave him Dr. Mather's Treatise of Tithes.

1708: And Alas! Alas! seventh-day Decr. 18, News is brought that the poor Child is Dead about an hour by sun *mane*. Alas! that I should fail seeing him alive! Now I went too late, save to weep with my Children, and kiss, and mourn over my dear Grandson. My son desired me to pray with his family; which I did. Madam Dudley, the Govrs Lady, Mrs. Katharin, and Mrs. Mary came in while I was there; and brought my little Rebekah with them. Call'd at the Governour's as came home. Seem to agree to bury the child next fourth day. I mention'd its being best to bury at Roxbury, for my son to keep to his own parish. Govr said I might put the Child in his father's Grave if I pleas'd. Got home well in my slay, had much adoe to avoid Slews. *Laus Deo*.

My son perceiving the Governour's aversion to have the child buried at Roxbury, writes to me of it. I go to the Governour's on Tuesday, and speak about Bearers, He leaves it to me; so does my son; as I come home I speake for Sir Ruggles, Timothy Ruggles, son of Martha Woodbridge, my ancient acquaintance and Townswoman; and Col. Checkley's son for the other. Wednesday, Decr 22, 1708. My dear Grandson, Sam Sewall, is buried; Son and daughter went first: Then Govr and I; then Madam Dudley led by Paul Dudley esqr; Then Joseph and Hanah; Then Mr. Wm. Dudley and daughter Hirst—Major Gen and his Lady here with their Coach—Mr. Bromfield, Stoddard &c. Gave Mr. Walter a Lutestring scarf, Bearers, Capt. Noyes, Mrs. Bayley, scarves. Decr. 30. Daughter Hirst is much oppress'd with a Fear of Death; desires to speak with me: I go to her presently after Lecture, and discourse with her, and she seems better compos'd.

Jany 24th. 1706-7 James Bayley Esqr. Ring and Glov[es].

[Years of Age] April, 23. *feria quarta*, The Reverd and pious Mr. Samuel Torrey; Gloves.

86. May, 12, 1707. Mrs. Lydia Scottow, Scarf and Gloves. 86 years old.

69. Decr. 4. 1707. The Honble F. J. Winthrop, Governour of Conecticut. Scarf, Ring, Gloves, Escutcheon. Gov. W. Tomb. Decr. 12. Mrs. Mary Eliot, widow of my dear friend Capt.

75. Jacob Eliot, and her self a very good woman. Scarf and Gloves.   75.

64. March, 22. 1707-8 Mrs. Sarah Noyes; Scarf and Gloves.

54. Augt. 17. 1708. Mrs. Mary Stoddard; Scarf and Ring.

73. Octobr. 20. 1708. Capt. Anthony Checkley, Scarf and Gloves.

76. Febr. 11th 1708-9 Mrs. Hanah Glover, Scarf and Gloves.

69. April, 30. 1709. James Russel Esqr. Scarf and Gloves. May, 6. Mrs. Abigail Russel his widow. Scarf, Gloves.

64. May, 9. Major Thomas Brown, of Sudbury, Esqr Scarf and Gloves.

80. May, 26. Mrs. Sarah Pemberton, Scarf and Gloves.

74. June, 8. Mrs. Ruth Wyllys, Scarf, Gloves.

55. July, 26. Mr. Thomas Banister, Scarf and Gloves.

61. January, 10 1709-10 Mr. John Hubbard; Scarf and Gloves.

63. Mrs. Elizabeth Savage, April, 16, 1710, Scarf and Gloves.

84. Madam———Stoddard, July, 19, 1710. Scarf and Gloves.

72. Isaac Goose, Decr. 2. 1710. Scarf and Gloves.

58. John Foster esqr, Febr. 15. Scarf, Ring, Gloves, Escutcheon.

40. Mrs. Anne Allen, Febr. 28 1710-11, Scarf and Gloves.

68. Mrs. Abigail Foster; March, 8. 1710-11, Scarf, Ring, Gloves, Escut.

57. Mrs. Sarah Banister, July, 3. 1711. Scarf and Ring, Gloves.

60. Mr. Elizur Holyoke, Augt. 14. 1711. Scarf and Gloves.

72. Mrs. Mary Ardel, Octobr 20. 1711. Scarf and Gloves. Mr. John Pole, Novr. 10. 1711. Scarf, Gloves, Escutcheon. Mrs. Margaret Corwin Decr. 3. Scarvs and Gloves.

73. Mrs. M. —— Atkinson, Jany. 4. Scarvs and Gloves.

69. Jno Walley Esqr., Jany. 17. Scarf, Ring, Gloves, Escutcheon.

77. John Fayerwether, Capt.   Scarf and Gloves. Apr. 14. 1712. Mrs. Elisa Whetcomb Augt 20. 1712. Scarf and Gloves.

80. Mrs. Sarah More, Novr. 26. Scarf and Gloves.

70. Samuel Hayman esqr. Decr. 18. Scarf and Gloves.

70. Mrs. Elisa Hutchinson Feb. 7. 1712, 13. Scarf, Ring, Gloves, Escut. Fun. Sermon.

76. Mrs. Elisa. Addington, March, 5th. Scarf, Ring, Gloves.

6-. Mrs. Elisa. Stoddard Apr. 22. 1713. Scarf, good Ring, Gloves, Scutcheon.

6-. Mrs. Martha Patteshall Apr. 23. Scarf and Gloves. Old B. place.

Mr. Thomas Brattle May, 21.

Col. Hunt.

Madam Bridget Usher's Funeral, May, 1723.

June	5.	To James Williams, Palls, Bells, &c	£1	8	6
		To Michael Haverblaton (?) & Comp, Porters	2	15	0
June	6.	To Mr. Leonard Cotton, Cancell'd his Bond, &c,	50	0	0
,,	8.	To the Rev. Mr. Benja. Wadsworth, his Legacy,	8	0	0
		To the Rev. Mr. Francis Foxcroft, ditto,	8	0	0
,,	10.	To John Blake, for three Coaches to Braintree, in service of the Funeral, May 30,	3	15	0
,,	11.	To Deacon Jn.° Marion, the Legacy given the poor of the Old Church,	4	0	0
		To Elisa. Hatch to 12 Duz. Glooves, at 4.	28	16	0
,,	12.	To Mr. John Edwards, 23 Rings	23	2	0
		To Eben Winbern, his Note, and Trunk, and Labour,	1	8	0
,,	15.	To Mr. John Read, a Retaining Fee, for Madam Usher's Executors,	0	10	0
		To Mr. Leonard Cotton, his and Mr. Oakes' Travelling Charges, May 28.	2	17	4
		To Nathan[1] Morse, Mad. Grove's Ring, 2 p. 18 Grains	1	13	0
		To Ema Salter, service for the Funeral,	0	6	0
,,	17.	To Mr. Robert Robinson, a Retaining Fee, for Mad. Usher's Executors,	0	10	0
,,	,,	To William Pain, for the Coffin,	3	0	0
June	23.	To Mr. Nathaniel Williams, Physician	4	10	0
,,	25.	To proving George Nowell's Bond, Witnesses 2, Justice, 2,	0	4	0
,,	26.	To an Attested Copy of the Will, of Mr. Secret.	0	2	6
		To John Marshall, of Braintree for the Grave and Monument,	24	10	0
,,	29.	Jane Bowdry, her Legacy,	1	0	0

July	6.	To Jno. Clark, Esq. Embowelling and Ceros,	4	0	0
,,	11.	To Printer Green, for inserting the Adver. three weeks successively, and 3 N. Letters,	0	5	9
,,	16.	To Col. Checkley, Recording her Death and Burial,	0	1	0
,,	29.	To Edward Oakes, in full,	16	0	0
Aug.	9.	To S. Kneeland, printing Mr. Foxcroft's Sermon, 4-1/2 sheets,	5	12	0

Puritans, as most men in the 17th century, believed that after death would come a new life of the spirit. The most popular account of that hope was Michael Wigglesworth's long and graphic poem, The Day of Doom *(Boston, 1662).*

15

The Mountains smoak, the Hills are shook,
   the Earth is rent and torn,
As if she should be clean dissolv'd,
   or from the Center born.
The Sea doth roar, forsakes the shore,
   and Shrinks away for fear;
The wild Beasts flee into the Sea,
   so soon as he draws near.

16

Whose Glory bright, whose wondrous might,
   whose Power Imperial,
So far surpass whatever was
   in Realms Terrestrial;
That tongues of men (nor Angels pen)
   cannot the same express,
And therefore I must pass it by,
   lest speaking should transgress.

17

Before his Throne a Trump is blown,
   Proclaiming th' Day of Doom:
Forthwith he cries, *Ye Dead arise,*
   and unto Judgment come.
No sooner said, but 'tis obey'd;
   Sepulchers open'd are:
Dead Bodies all rise at his call,
   and's mighty power declare.

18

Both Sea and Land, at his Command,
   their Dead at once surrender:
The Fire and Air constrained are
   also their dead to tender.
The mighty word of this great Lord
   links Body and Soul together
Both of the Just, and the unjust,
   to part no more for ever.

19

The same translates, from Mortal states
   to Immortality,
All that survive, and be alive,
   i' th' twinkling of an eye:
That so they may abide for ay
   to endles weal or woe;
Both the Renate and Reprobate
   are made to dy no more.

20

His winged Hosts file through all Coasts,
   together gathering
Both good and bad, both quick and dead,
   and all to Judgment bring.

Out of their holes those creeping Moles,
    that hid themselves for fear,
By force they take, and quickly make
    before the Judge appear.

21

Thus every one before the Throne
    of Christ the Judge is brought,
Both righteous and impious
    that good or ill had wrought.
A separation, and diff'ring station
    by Christ appointed is
(To sinners sad) 'twixt good and bad,
    'twixt Heirs of woe and bliss.

22

At Christ's right hand the Sheep do stand,
    his holy Martyrs, who
For his dear Name suffering shame,
    calamity and woe,
Like Champions stood, and with their Blood
    their testimony sealed;
Whose innocence without offence,
    to Christ their Judge appealed.

23

Next unto whom there find a room
    all Christ's afflicted ones,
Who being chastised, neither despised
    nor sank amidst their groans:
Who by the Rod were turn'd to G d,
    and loved him the more,
Not murmuring nor quarrelling
    when they were chast'ned sore.

24

Moreover, such as loved much,
   that had not such a tryal,
As might constrain to so great pain,
   and such deep self-denyal:
Yet ready were the Cross to bear,
   when Christ them call'd thereto,
And did rejoyce to hear his voice,
   they're counted Sheep also.

25

Christ's Flock of Lambs there also stands,
   whose Faith was weak, yet true;
All sound Believers (Gospel receivers)
   whose Grace was small, but grew:
And them among an Infant throng
   of Babes, for whom Christ dy'd;
Whom for his own, by wayes unknown
   to men, he sanctify'd.

26

All stand before their Saviour
   in long white Robes yclad,
Their countenance full of pleasance,
   appearing wondrous glad.
O glorious sight! Behold how bright
   dust heaps are made to shine,
Conformed so their Lord unto,
   whose Glory is Divine.

27

At Christ's left hand the Goats do stand,
   all whining hypocrites,
Who for self-ends did seem Christ's friends,
   but foster'd guileful sprites;
Who Sheep resembled, but they dissembled
   (their hearts were not sincere);

Who once did throng Christ's Lambs among,
   but now must not come near.

28

Apostates and Run-awayes,
   such as have Christ forsaken,
Of whom the Devil, with seven more evil,
   hath fresh possession taken:
Sinners in grain, reserv'd to pain
   and torments most severe:
Because 'gainst light they sinn'd with spight,
   are also placed there.

29

There also stand a num'rous band,
   that no Profession made
Of Godliness, nor to redress
   their wayes at all essay'd:
Who better knew, but (sinful Crew)
   Gospel and Law despised;
Who all Christ's knocks withstood like blocks
   and would not be advised.

30

Moreover, there with them appear
   a number, numberless
Of great and small, vile wretches all,
   that did Gods Law transgress:
Idolaters, false worshippers,
   Prophaners of Gods Name,
Who not at all thereon did call,
   or took in vain the same.

31

Blasphemers lewd, and Swearers shrewd,
    Scoffers at Purity,
That hated God, contemn'd his Rod,
    and lov'd Security;
Sabbath-polluters, Saints persecutors,
    Presumptuous men and proud,
Who never lov'd those that reprov'd;
    all stand amongst this Crowd.

32

Adulterers and Whoremongers
    were there, with all unchast:
There Covetous, and Ravenous,
    that Riches got too fast:
Who us'd vile ways themselves to raise
    t' Estates and worldly wealth,
Oppression by, or Knavery,
    by force, or fraud, or stealth.

33

Moreover, there together were
    Children flagitious,
And Parents who did them undo
    by Nurture vicious.
False-witness-bearers, and self-foreswearers,
    Murd'rers, and Men of blood,
Witches, Inchanters, and Ale-house-haunters,
    beyond account there stood.

34

Their place there find all Heathen blind,
    that Natures light abused,
Although they had no tydings glad,
    of Gospel-grace refused.

There stands all Nations and Generations
   of *Adam's* Progeny,
Whom Christ redeem'd not, who Christ esteem'd not,
   through Infidelity.

35

Who no Peace-maker, no Undertaker,
   to shrow'd them from Gods ire,
Ever obtain'd; they must be pained
   with everlasting fire.
These num'rous bands, wringing their hands,
   and weeping, all stand there,
Filled with anguish, whose hearts do languish
   through self-tormenting fear.

36

Fast by them stand at Christ's left hand
   the Lion fierce and fell,
The Dragon bold, that Serpent old,
   that hurried Souls to Hell.
There also stand, under command,
   Legions of Sprights unclean,
And hellish Fiends, that are no friends
   to God, nor unto Men.

37

With dismal chains, and strongest reins,
   like Prisoners of Hell,
They're held in place before Christ's face,
   till He their Doom shall tell.
These void of tears, but fill'd with fears,
   and dreadful expectation
Of endless pains, and scalding flames,
   stand waiting for Damnation.

38

All silence keep, both Goats and Sheep,
   before the Judge's Throne;
With mild aspect to his Elect
   then spake the Holy One:
My Sheep draw near, your Sentence hear,
   which is to you no dread,
Who clearly now discern, and know
   your sins are pardoned. . . .

48

Come, Blessed Ones, and sit on Thrones,
   Judging the World with me:
Come, and possess your happiness,
   and bought felicitie.
Henceforth no fears, no care, no tears,
   no sin shall you annoy,
Nor any thing that grief doth bring:
   Eternal Rest enjoy. . . .

51

The wicked are brought to the Bar,
   like guilty Malefactors,
That oftentimes of bloody Crimes
   and Treasons have been Actors.
Of wicked Men, none are so mean
   as there to be neglected:
Nor none so high in dignity,
   as there to be respected.

52

The glorious Judge will priviledge
   nor Emperour, nor King:
But every one that hath mis-done
   doth into Judgment bring.

And every one that hath mis-done,
   the Judge impartially
Condemneth to eternal wo,
   and endless misery. . . .

205

They wring their hands, their caitiff-hands
   and gnash their teeth for terrour;
They cry, they roar for anguish sore,
   and gnaw their tongues for horrour.
But get away without delay,
   Christ pitties not your cry:
Depart to Hell, there may you yell,
   and roar Eternally.

206

That word, *Depart*, maugre their heart,
   drives every wicked one,
With mighty pow'r, the self-same hour,
   far from the Judge's Throne.
Away they're chaste by the strong blast
   of his Death-threatning mouth:
They flee full fast, as if in haste,
   although they be full loath.

207

As chaff that's dry, and dust doth fly
   before the Northern wind:
Right so are they chased away,
   and can no Refuge find.
They hasten to the Pit of Wo,
   guarded by Angels stout;
Who to fulfil Christ's holy will,
   attend this wicked Rout.

208

Whom having brought, as they are taught,
    unto the brink of Hell,
(That dismal place far from Christ's face,
    where Death and Darkness dwell:
Where Gods fierce Ire kindleth the fire,
    and vengeance feefs the flame
With piles of Wood, and Brimstone Flood,
    that none can quench the same,)

209

With Iron bands they bind their hands,
    and cursed feet together,
And cast them all, both great and small,
    into that Lake for ever.
Where day and night, without respite,
    they wail, and cry, and howl
For tort'ring pain, which they sustain
    in Body and in Soul.

210

For day and night, in their despight,
    their torments smoak ascendeth.
Their pain and grief have no relief,
    their anguish never endeth.
There must they ly, and never dy,
    though dying every day:
There must they dying ever ly,
    and not consume away.

211

Dy fain they would, if dy they could,
    but Death will not be had:
God's direful wrath their bodies hath
    for ev'r Immortal made.

They live to ly in misery,
 and bear eternal wo;
And live they must whilst God is just,
 that he may plague them so. . . .